The Tell-All Guide to Airbnb Hosting

Proven Tips and Tricks for Successful Hosting

Deborah Voll

"Ms. Voll's storytelling on being an Airbnb Superhost is spot on. Not only does this pithy volume relate the frustrations, annoyances, and—at times—horrors of hosting strangers in your home, it includes the delights of welcoming, getting to know, and—in some cases—becoming good friends with people from all over the world. Her insightful key points provide tips for would-be hosts as well as questions to consider before taking the plunge. A must read for anyone thinking about becoming a host."

—S. A. Snyder, Airbnb Superhost and Author of *Plant Trees, Carry Sheep: A Woman's Spiritual Journey Among the Sufis of Scotland*

"Deborah Voll's book is very well written and has great tips for guests and hosts alike!"

—Gwen Satterfield, Middle School Math Teacher, FLVS, and Airbnb frequent guest

"Author Deborah Voll offers a masterclass on how to be an Airbnb host (and guest). This book is not only helpful to the wanna be host, but would also be valuable to those who are already hosting and seek to improve their guests' experiences. As someone who always stays in hotels, this book has piqued my curiosity about the Airbnb experience. Voll not only discusses such mundane things as keeping a plunger handy in guest bathrooms, providing a supply of half-n-half for coffee in the fridge, but also the likelihood that the host and guest will develop a friendship. Voll's personal stories make this an enjoyable read."

—Katharine M. Nohr, Host of "The Wide World of Esports" on ThinkTech Hawaii

The Tell-All Guide to Airbnb Hosting

Proven Tips and Tricks for Successful Hosting

Deborah Voll

Green Bay, WI

Publisher/Executive Editor: Brittiany Koren
Copy-editor: A.L. Mundt
Cover Art Designer: Ed Vincent/ENC Graphics
Print Interior Layout Designer: Katy Brunette
Ebook Interior Layout Designer: Maria Connor

Category: Hospitality Self-Help Guide
Description: The ultimate guide to creating a profitable home sharing experience by an Airbnb host.
Paperback ISBN: 978-1-951375-42-3
Ebook ISBN: 978-1-951375-43-0
LOC Catalogue Data: Applied for.

First Edition published by Written Dreams Publishing in May, 2021.

Green Bay, WI 54311

Table of Contents

Preface

Since 2012, I have been a regular host on the Airbnb site. As of September 2020, I have hosted 942 guests from eighteen countries, starting with one room then two. Through this transition, my space and the privacy in my home have shrunk, but my life experiences have grown.

Most travelers who stay with me are curious about my hosting life and ask what it's like to host people in your home and share a space on a regular basis. They are always curious about some of the challenges of hosting, too. I find that people are interested in human nature and the home-sharing concept and wonder about the challenging and rewarding aspects of the job.

Over the years, I've also been surprised by people who make assumptions that this is an easy job or a quick way to make money. They believe that you simply put a bed in a corner with some sheets and a pillow and call it good. Being a host in any type of home-sharing platform is a far larger commitment when you decide to host people in your own home, rather than offsite in an apartment or condo.

On several occasions, I've also been asked to help others start their own hosting business on the Airbnb platform. It's been fun to see them succeed in their endeavor while showing them successful tricks for managing guests and the Airbnb platform itself.

This book is specifically for anyone who is interested in becoming an Airbnb host, particularly with in-house guests. You will learn some do's and don'ts of being a great host, the common issues and scenarios you may experience and how to overcome them, and my pro tips to avoid some common pitfalls when you start your hosting adventure. I also share my own stories and lessons I've learned the hard way regarding hosting (and myself), which may entertain you as an added bonus.

Airbnb is continually making changes to their platform to enhance the experience for hosts and guests. Any data provided is accurate as written, but some mentioned features or rules may be updated or changed by Airbnb at any time, as companies are prone to do. The experiences and advice shared in this book are timeless.

I hope you'll sit back and enjoy the journey!

Chapter 1

The Beginning of the Journey

Imagine a crisp summer Seattle day in July 2018. The temperature was an unusual eighty degrees, "the mountain was out" as we say in Seattle, and Lake Washington had warmed up enough so that if you went paddle boarding and fell in, you wouldn't freeze! This was my evening to meet my good friend for an after-work paddleboard excursion, which is often hard to fit in with both our schedules. We work full time and each run our own Airbnb. After a couple of hours of boarding, she attempted to entice me with a glass of wine on the deck, but I declined and headed home since there were things to do around the house. Driving home and feeling grateful for the afterwork splurge, I felt relaxed from getting a good dunk in the lake and a dose of vitamin D.

Now picture the following: I walked into my home and in the kitchen were my two guests lounging at the counter while a FIRE was starting on the stovetop! Consider how you might first react had it been your spouse, sibling, or kid. Now think how you might have to hold your composure if it was a paying guest in your home who had a language barrier as well. As for me, I did my best to pull myself together, took a deep breath, and walked in.

The son spoke English but the mother did not. She didn't know that a ceramic stovetop is still hot enough to catch paper on fire after it's turned off.

I was direct, yet courteous with both, but the mother felt embarrassed. I politely told the son that any additional cooking in the home would need to be done while I was in the home. They understood. None of us wanted my home to burn down, and they were staying for another five days.

Welcome to the Airbnb host experience!

People are often baffled that I rent out two rooms in my home via Airbnb and ask how I started. They want to know what my motivation was since having strangers in your home invades privacy. It's a long story filled with a lot of history and background, and the journey has been an experience filled with ups and downs. I've learned a lot of lessons along the way in regard to myself, my family, and my Airbnb community.

It's interesting that some people still have not heard of Airbnb nor used the concept of home sharing in their travels. Boy, are they missing the boat.

Airbnb first started in 2008 by three gentlemen—Brian Chesky, Joe Gebbia, and Nathan Blecharczyk. Living in San Francisco, they were hard-pressed to pay their upcoming rent. A design conference was coming to San Francisco in late October, and they knew the industry personally, so they decided to create a bed-and-breakfast for some conference members using the empty space in their apartment. They called the service AirBed and Breakfast and booked three guests—two shared a room and one stayed in the kitchen on an air mattress. They even provided pop tarts and orange juice for their guests. That one weekend earned them $1,000. The Airbnb concept began as a resource for finding available rooms during sold-out conferences across the country and developed into what we experience today.[1]

Some time ago, Chesky wrote that as society

---

1   Gallagher, Leigh. *The Airbnb Story: How Three Ordinary Guys Disrupted an Industry, Made Billions . . . and Created Plenty of Controversy.* Boston, MA: MARINER Books, 2018.

became industrialized, the personal feeling was being replaced with mass produced and often impersonal travel experiences, and people stopped trusting one another. Airbnb would stand for something much bigger than travel; it would stand for community and relationships and use technology to bring people together. Airbnb would be the one place people could go to meet the universal human yearning to belong. By "belonging," he meant for people to venture out in places and neighborhoods that they might not have chosen to stay in prior to the Airbnb experience.[2]

As of September 2020, Airbnb has 5.6 million listings in 100,000 cities and 220 countries with Tokyo, New York City, and Paris as the top three most requested cities.[3] Airbnb went public at the end of 2020 with a valuation of 75 billion dollars,[4] and the four million hosts have earned more than 110 billion dollars while hosting 800 million guests.[5] Travelers often use the site because of the affordability of the homes or rooms, the locations, and the experiences. I keep saying the order is price, experience, then location! A hotel room is so boring, and for the most part, they look the same.

However, when you stay in someone's home, they may greet you at the door and show you your room, then perhaps offer you a glass of wine—that's not a personal touch you get when you check in to a hotel. It's a host's personal touch and the level of care and concern for travelers that make the Airbnb

2   Chesky, Brian. "Belong Anywhere." The Airbnb Blog. July 18, 2014. Accessed March 10, 2019. https://blog.atairbnb.com/belong-anywhere/.

3   Airbnb. "About Us." Airbnb Newsroom, September 30, 2020. Accessed January 12, 2021. https://news.airbnb.com/about-us/.

4   Team, Trefis. "Making Sense Of Airbnb Stock's $75 Billion Valuation." Forbes. Forbes Magazine, December 17, 2020. Accessed January 12, 2021. https://www.forbes.com/sites/greatspeculations/2020/12/17/making-sense-of-airbnb-stocks-75-billion-valuation/?sh=6d0f01fe1adb.

5   Airbnb. "About Us." Airbnb Newsroom, September 30, 2020. Accessed January 12, 2021. https://news.airbnb.com/about-us/.

experience unique. For those who want a larger space to accommodate a larger group, there are whole home or condo rentals available, and you'll find some of the same unique touches of care. Both options are fantastic because they offer the guest the option of affordability, location, and experience. All are important, in my book, when traveling.

How did I get started as a host on Airbnb? I'd heard of the home-sharing platform on a blog I read and decided that a trip to San Francisco in 2012 for a friend's birthday might be a good chance to experience the site and see what the buzz was all about. I was a single mom, and at the time, my children were old enough to stay home alone, so I just needed a room for myself. I love to explore cities and had an event to attend, so I wouldn't be in my room much. It was the perfect opportunity to give it a try!

I had booked a room with a shared bath. The house was in the perfect location based on where I wanted to be in the city, and the pictures on the site proved to be accurate. My host worked during the day, so I had a self-check-in process and didn't even see her until checkout on Monday morning.

We had a chance to visit at breakfast, and I asked her how she got started with hosting and what she liked and didn't like about it. She encouraged me to try the platform. Since I was single, with college-bound kids and a need for extra money, I gave it some serious consideration before deciding it was worth a shot.

December 29, 2012, our first guest from Auckland, New Zealand arrived. I had moved all personal items out of the master bedroom and bathroom to make way for a comfortable experience for the incoming guest. Everything came out of drawers, clothes were moved out of closets, medicine cabinets were emptied, and all personal effects were removed. Family pictures were replaced and other decorative touches updated. I moved all my belongings to my daughter's room across the hall since she was away at college.

I'm sure this guest had no idea how nervous I was before he walked through the door! So nervous, in fact, that I had to have a glass of wine prior to his arranged arrival which was at two in the afternoon. What was I doing inviting a stranger in my home with a high school son in a bedroom across the hall? I second-guessed myself that entire afternoon.

In my opinion, each detail had to be just perfect for the guest. I knew from the Airbnb site that reviews meant everything, and a bad review right out of the gate meant a demise of my future as a host on the site.

I'm happy to say that he was a great guest, and the whole visit went smoothly. Although, I don't recall letting my son talk the entire weekend as I feared he might be too loud or obnoxious. We took our dog, Ginger, in the car with us everywhere we went because we were concerned how she might react to a stranger coming and going from the house. This was a learning curve for the entire family. Looking back, it's comical to remember that first weekend and how we tried so hard to make sure the guest's experience ran perfectly. Despite any concerns I had, we got a glowing review, and he even booked with us again on a return trip.

We have also used the platform as travelers, which has been great fun to see other listings, connect with other hosts, share experiences, and learn tips to make us better hosts. Since 2012, I've stayed in twenty-five places, some in the United States and some internationally. I've enjoyed some incredible experiences and met unforgettable people.

Once my family thought it would be fun to stay in a tiny house, so we booked one in the Seattle area. Another time, my son and I stayed in a replica wildfire lookout tower in Tiller, Oregon, and had an amazing time with two wonderful hosts. We've been to California and rented homes on the ocean and enjoyed weekend excursions elsewhere in Washington state. My trip to London and Paris was made possible because we rented flats in both London and Paris, which made the entire trip more affordable and fun as it offered us the local flair of the neighborhoods. We were able to experience restaurants and places that we may not have seen otherwise if we had stayed in a downtown hotel.

Thanks to hosting and traveling, I've learned a lot from my own experiences and from others. Now when my kids book their own vacations, I always ask them "What made that place so special? What can we do to incorporate that into our shared space?"

In the following chapters, I will be sharing those experiences with you. They are tips and tricks that you can incorporate into your own hosting business. You may have heard the saying by Carl W. Beuhner, "They may forget what you said—but they will never forget how you made them feel." I try to incorporate that sentiment with every guest experience in my home and I hope you will, too.

Chapter 2

Your Time Is Not Your Time

If you're thinking of becoming an Airbnb host, you need to realize that your time will no longer be your time, and you must set boundaries and navigate them. I learned a few things right away: when you are hosting, especially rooms in your current home, guests may arrive with lots of questions, or you will receive a reservation request or inquires that need a quick response. Often these situations occur at an inconvenient time.

As a host, you have committed to getting back to an inquiry online within twenty-four hours to accept or decline it. Inquiries can come in at any hour of the day. You have twenty-four hours to respond, but the host who responds first and answers any questions a potential guest may have is the one who books the guest. This is critical when you first start out as a host.

I've been on my way to a river rafting trip in southern Oregon or heading into a movie theater and had inquiries that needed a response. Fortunately, the mobile app is convenient for quick responses, but you must still pay attention to the guest details on the app and not rush into accepting an inquiry without reviewing the full details. You could book two people and an infant when your profile states your room is suitable for only one person! Yes, it's happened.

Consider your last Fourth of July holiday. Was the

sun shining, did you have a picnic at the park, or get up early to watch the parade? On my last Fourth of July in Seattle, the sun was shining on a gorgeous day, but I had to wait until two guests checked out before I could spend the remainder of the day flipping both of the rooms for the next incoming guests.

What is *flipping a room*? Some people may use another term, but flipping a room in our home entails washing all the bed linens and towels, cleaning the bathroom, dusting, vacuuming, and making sure the room is spotless for the next guest. That next guest may be arriving in a matter of hours.

If you are lucky enough, you'll have a guest who was considerate of the room and tidy. However, if not, you may work for some time to make sure the room passes the white glove test. One time, I had a guest who stayed with me for a couple of weeks and had many items shipped to our home, without asking I might add. When he left, all the empty boxes were piled in the room. I had to break down all of the boxes before I could even start to clean the room. I certainly lost a lot of my time during that flip.

So, back to that Fourth of July, it wasn't until the next guest checked in at 4:30 p.m. that I was able to sit down outside and enjoy the remainder of the holiday. You need to anticipate that there are going to be days or times when you'd rather be doing an activity with friends or relaxing, but duty calls. Frequently, once I get home from work on a Friday evening, I am cleaning a bathroom and thinking of my other friends who may be going out for dinner or catching a movie. Then I remember my *why*.

To do this type of hosting, you need to have a firm reason for why you are doing this. Is it to save for a vacation, pay for college tuition, install new gutters on the house, or put on a new roof? These were a lot of my *whys* when I started, and they kept me going when I was home alone cleaning toilets.

If I can, I try to squeeze in a couple more errands or

an evening walk before a guest arrives. On a Saturday while waiting for people to check out, I'll create a list of things that need to be done so that I'm making the most of my time while playing the waiting game. If the guest is lucky, three old bananas will be on the counter waiting to be turned into banana bread. Since Airbnb does not require hosts to provide meals, it's a fun surprise for a guest to come down in the morning and be offered a slice or two of my freshly made banana bread. It's a great tip to get the house smelling cozy, too!

Our check-in policy is after four p.m. for reasons related to getting people checked out and the room prepared for the next check-in. When I began hosting, my son and I would stay awake until ungodly hours in the morning waiting to greet people and give them that warm hospitality welcome. Often, a guest would fly in, get their car, and decide to go out to dinner before checking in, forgetting or not caring about the specified time for check-in. It's for those reasons that we put a lockbox on the house. If it's after nine p.m. or we know they'll be late, the guests are given self-check-in instructions. That way, no one is left waiting or rushing to get to their room. This is a standard system for most hosts now. I will add, though, that a guest will feel a lot more comfortable with you and your home if you have welcomed them or had someone step in to greet them. Sometimes that is not realistic, but you should strive to be present.

There have been several times when I've been invited to go on a weekend or day trip with friends, and I've had to decline because I needed to flip a room that day or had a guest check in. Other times, I have employed a service or friend to come in and help flip a room if I am unable to be home or have a unique situation. Having an alternative back-up plan to help in case of emergencies is important to make sure the entire hosting experience runs smoothly.

The home-sharing concept has sparked a lot of

side businesses in the industry. There are people who specifically solicit Airbnb hosts to offer cleaning services for their rooms or homes. It's a unique niche and one that has become quite handy for many hosts, especially those with separate rental locations.

The beauty of the Airbnb site is that you do have the flexibility to block out certain periods of time if you want to go somewhere, or want to have the home to yourself for a family occasion, or just need a break. I'm frequently asked, "Why don't you have a permanent boarder in your home? Then you know who it is, and you don't need to do the check-in and checkout."

My response is always the same: I enjoy meeting new people and establishing relationships. If I have a bad guest, they will leave soon, and I don't have to allow them to re-book. If a long-term boarder is unpleasant, you are stuck with them!

Recently, I had a couple from Europe stay with me for several weeks. They were quite lovely; however, every morning I knew they were on vacation because of their extracurricular activities in bed. It caused embarrassment for us as their hosts, and we were glad when they moved on. Perhaps they didn't realize how loud they were, though I did remind them a couple of times that my room was below theirs.

In the remaining chapters, I'll share both good and difficult guest experiences, and how I dealt with each one. As a host, you never know what type of experience you and the guest will have in your space. Being optimistic about a good experience is the key to success.

<u>Key Points to Remember</u>

- Be responsive to your potential guests. Your response to the inquiry, in both timing and politeness, will result in their decision to book with you or not. You must establish yourself as trustworthy, caring, and responsible.

- What is your *why*? During those tough moments, what will keep you focused on why you are doing this crazy, exciting, new venture?

- Have a simple and straightforward procedure for late check-ins or when you can't be there to greet them.

- Make sure you allow plenty of time for flipping rooms and your own personal schedule. Set your boundaries and stick to them.

Chapter 3

Patience

Before committing to the Airbnb hosting platform, I wouldn't have considered myself a patient person. I wanted things completed right away, hurried people along, disliked standing in line—which usually happened! Maybe as I got older, I've developed more patience for people and situations, but I have to owe a lot of my development of patience to being a host.

Every day people log on to the Airbnb site in search of new experiences. I found that in the early days of Airbnb, the company didn't do much to set the right expectations for what was required of a potential guest. Potential customers would reach out to book a room without a profile picture uploaded for the host to view who they were. Would you let a stranger in your home without seeing a picture of them first? There is a comfort level in seeing a guest's picture that helps develop a trusting relationship. Posting a picture of a dog, rainbow, or a cartoon character doesn't let that relationship begin properly, either.

If I do receive a request without an accurate picture, I request that the potential guest updates it so that I am comfortable with whom I'm speaking regarding the listing. Most guests have no issues with obliging that request.

Many times, a guest tries to book a room without uploading their credit card information, which allows the booking to be confirmed and processed. Without it, the booking process stalls and potentially prevents another guest from booking the room. This issue is expected to be addressed in updates for 2021 to ensure any attempts to book will require a credit card.

Sometimes, a potential customer attempts to book a room for a family member coming to town. This may seem a perfectly acceptable situation, so why is this an issue? As hosts, our online profiles make house rules and basic information concerning the home extremely clear. Once a person inquires and we accept, we hold the guest accountable to those rules. If someone else books a room for a family member, the opportunity to establish that relationship with the actual guest prior to their arrival is lost, and the actual guest may not clearly understand or accept the house rules.

I've had to practice a lot of patience in these instances when I felt I was constantly teaching new people how to use the site. Why is all of this important? Because I've been asked, "How do you know if you even want to accept a reservation request from someone?"

A lot of the decision-making process is a gut feeling based on a guest's profile, their previous reviews (which should always be read), and their purpose for coming to the area. These items are taken into account when deciding whether or not to accept a reservation.

Have I ever declined a reservation? Sure, but in the years I have been hosting, the declined requests have been a result of the guest not putting enough information in their profile or not communicating clearly about their request. Every host is different, but I base my decision on the information the guest provides.

Some hosts may accept any applicant in an effort to keep their rental booked continuously. When I am a guest, I reach out and provide enough information as to who is coming with me on the trip and the purpose for our visit. Why not establish a good impression on the front end? And as a host, taking the time to walk a potential guest through the application process is an easy way to practice some patience in hopes of having a better guest/host experience during their stay.

Remember the mother and son guests at the beginning who started a fire on the stovetop in my home? During the balance of their stay, I had to have an extra dose of patience. When they first arrived, they didn't know how to work any of the appliances, so I held a brief tutorial, but clearly, it was not in-depth enough. Unfortunately, we had a language barrier combined with a lack of experience with modern appliances, which challenged both parties.

That first morning, as I was ready to walk out the door, the young man wanted to cook breakfast on the stove and didn't have the faintest idea on how to use the range. I came back in and spent ten minutes with him helping to cook his breakfast for his mom while he watched. Every morning, this young man would come down and make breakfast for himself and his mom. Towards the end of his stay, I asked him who did the cooking back home, and he responded that his grandmother cooked for the entire household.

I also had a guest, who I will refer to as Nancy, who stayed with us for a couple of months. She was an older, retired woman and was relocating to Seattle for a life change. You might think, as I did, an older person means responsible and quiet—a piece of cake! Well, I learned a lot of lessons from Nancy, but I'll put her in the patience category.

During the first week, Nancy was fine and abided by the house rules and seemed pleasant. I enjoyed her company since she was around a lot. Anytime I arrived home from work, she was there. After that, Nancy started to show her true colors. She began to rearrange the house, brought chairs from her storage shed into my house and put my furniture out in the garage!

She complained about everything, including that there was no lock on her bedroom door, but none of the rooms had locks—not even my own room. She informed me that I needed to bathe the dog more because she stank. Nancy was allergic to garlic, so we couldn't cook with garlic. The list went on.

My reviews have a great track record, so her complaints were nit-picky items. She even bought primroses in planting containers that she wanted to put in my front yard. She assumed that I would want to have her containers on my doorstep. I still shudder when I go to a nursery and see primroses in the spring.

After that first week, Nancy seemed to think of herself not as a guest but as a roommate or part owner of the property; however, she was staying temporarily. There are horror stories of people coming and never leaving in the hosting world. I was beginning to think that I had one such guest on my hands. She is the only guest I've ever hosted where I said out loud to her that if she was so unhappy, perhaps she should find other accommodations. But she wouldn't leave early, so I guess she wasn't unhappy!

I had to have a tremendous amount of patience because she was a challenge. The entire time she stayed, I had to remind myself daily of my *why*. At that time, the *why* was that I planned to take my daughter to London and Paris that year, and Nancy's revenue would pay for our Airbnb accommodations for two weeks. That plan kept us going despite the painful situation.

My friends and family were also patient since they often took the brunt of my venting phone calls. They can probably recollect more of the stories than I can at this point. Other experiences required patience, but none compared to my days with Nancy. All hosts (even hotels) will have at least one horror guest, and Nancy was mine.

When she finally departed at the end of her months-long stay, the communication and relationship was cordial but not friendly. She packed her belongings and her furniture and headed out the door without bothering to place my items back in their original locations. Nancy had an obvious disregard for my belongings and feelings. At that point, I didn't care. I had survived those months by reminding myself that this was only temporary and our trip to London was on the horizon!

Surprisingly, Nancy suggested towards the end of her stay that we not leave reviews for each other. I was fine with that suggestion. She drove into the sunset, and I put my house back together.

Another guest offered me opportunities for practicing patience. I had a summer intern from Surat, India, who was a great guest, but he would open the dishwasher and put his dirty dishes in it alongside the clean dishes. I finally put out a sign that said, "Clean Dishes in Dishwasher" but dirty dishes still appeared in the clean dishwasher. Several times, we had to run the dishes through the clean cycle again. Having lots of different guests with various cultural experiences can present its own set of challenges which requires tremendous patience. Expectations in regard to the cleanliness of the kitchen is only one example.

You will have guests who test your patience, and you will make it through because they are staying with you temporarily. Their needs come before your own, and it will likely happen at an inconvenient time. Giving that guest grace and patience is what you would want if you were a guest as well, right?

<u>Key Points to Remember</u>

- Read potential guest reviews before accepting their booking request. Always follow your gut feeling to make the final decision. Airbnb does not penalize you for declining a reservation request (at this time).

- Be up front with a guest who is more difficult than others. I did ask Nancy if she felt more comfortable finding a different space to rent. I gave her an option to leave, but she declined. I could have pushed the issue further but didn't want to antagonize her. You will have to decide how you would have reacted with a guest like her and choose your own course of action.

- Challenging guests are temporary.

- Patience is key not only with the situation but with yourself. I've learned many skills in these circumstances and discovered how quickly thoughts create our emotions which drive our actions. It's been a gamechanger for me!

Chapter 4

Letting Go of Perfection

As I mentioned before, I had to learn to develop patience when I became a host, and quite frankly, I'm still working on it. The same applies to me letting go of seeking perfection.

In our home, every guest deserves a comfortable and unique experience. As a host, I want to make sure that every part of the guest experience is perfect: the shower is spotless, the front step is vacuumed of pine needles, etc. Yes, I said *vacuumed*. It's a faster process than sweeping. Remember, we need to be efficient. Each item must pass the white glove test that I referred to earlier.

I learned that guests make assumptions as to what is acceptable to do in a home, and on occasion, I've had to bite my tongue and ask myself if the issue will matter in a couple more weeks. Some things are hard to let go of, and the subject of guest mail is a big bone of contention with me in our home.

I have had long- and short-term guests who feel that it's okay to have their online purchases shipped to our house and mail sent to the mailbox without asking. On occasion, I've come home from work and not been able to get through the door because there were huge boxes on the front doorstep that were too heavy for me to lift. I've had people buy bicycles, computers, and new luggage—all shipped to my house—so guests can take more things home. I wouldn't mind if they asked, but they rarely do.

I also get people who stay for a couple weeks, and they have their mail sent to my home. One guest had checked out six months prior, and I received their W-2 from their employer in my mailbox. How odd is that? Wouldn't their employer have their up-to-date address? And wouldn't the guest be concerned about such private information being sent to a temporary location? I would think so.

My poor mailman has been confused on several occasions. On the inside of our mailbox, I've written our family names and then "not so-and-so, or so-and-so." My mailman has come to my door and asked who these people are on the envelopes with my address. He kindly asked if I didn't want *any* mail delivered without our names on it. I had to explain the situation and instruct him that it's okay to leave the mail because I have had to let go of being bothered by the situation and allow guests to receive their mail at my home.

Keeping our home tidy is a constant process, and some people would say that I'm reaching for perfectionism. Our yard is extensive, and I've often found myself outside weeding the front gardens or cleaning up leaves prior to a guest's arrival. It's part of that first impression that I feel is important with a guest. When I'm a guest, if I arrive at my reservation and the house doesn't look well-kept or the yard is in shambles, I question what the inside is going to look like.

On the back patio, I keep the glass table and chairs clean in case a guest wants to sit in the garden and read or work on their computer. Depending on the weather, a person can't be out in twenty-eight degree weather doing yard maintenance, so it's one of those items where I've had to let go of perfection and move on.

I occasionally have guests who are interns for the summer and stay for several months. I strive to keep the kitchen cupboards tidy as well as clean out and wash the fridge on a regular rotation. Where I have learned to let go is when we have short- and long-term guests who buy food and don't eat it all or leave half-eaten food behind. This food can only be thrown in the trash. I can't tell you how often I've asked if the unknown pints of ice cream were my son's, only to throw them away because they weren't.

Our home was built in 1979 and over the years we've continued to update and maintain both the interior and exterior. I've been so fortunate to have the Airbnb revenue to help with a lot of home improvements. However, not every appliance and item of furniture has been updated. I had a guest once comment that we had a vintage microwave. Well, in fact, we did. It was a built-in wall unit and was installed with the original vintage oven. I'm happy to say that the vintage microwave got replaced recently.

As homeowners, it's obvious that we need to prioritize our home maintenance each year, but it's also important when you are hosting guests to make sure that the home maintenance is up to snuff. This should mean the gutters are not hanging off the roof, and basic repairs are done in a timely fashion. What you think can be put off may not be acceptable to a guest. Of course, safety issues need to be handled immediately.

The restroom is another place where I have to let it go in some instances. One of the house rules is that guests should use the squeegee to clean off the glass doors when they are done showering in the master bath. This is a good practice to keep the shower looking nice and maintain the space so it's easier to clean. For the most part, the guests adhere to the rule laminated on the shower door. I appreciate it when people take the extra time to do this small gesture.

We've had instances where some of our guests will handwash their clothes in the sink and hang them to dry. I attempted to let this go but have had to ask guests to allow me to handle their laundry because the excess water sitting in a pool on the counter ruins the finish and the floor. When it comes to damaging the rental space, I *don't* let it go. Instead, I find a solution or compromise that works for all of us and keeps my space functional for future guests.

For guests who are staying for a longer length of time, I clean the room and bathroom weekly. Sometimes it's easy, and other times I shake my head at the amount of clutter and filth when I can't even get to the bathroom counter. But it's important to tidy their area without jeopardizing their privacy. I have to tell myself to let go of the perfection and do the best I can based on the situation and hope that they are appreciative of the effort.

I once had an international guest who checked in late in the evening. It was his first time in the U.S. He retired to his room but soon had to alert me when the toilet overflowed! Fortunately, I had a good plumber on call who came to fix it and mentioned two things: too much toilet paper had been used, and I needed to tell the guest to refrain from using so much paper. I'm sure you can imagine that conversation. The plumber's bill was more than double what I would receive from the guest for his two-night stay. I had to let it go and chalk it up to experience. Hopefully without a lot of embarrassment, the guest learned a valuable lesson. His future Airbnb hosts can thank me!

On the subject of using restrooms, some guests will take a thirty-to-forty-minute shower. I don't time my own showers, so I'm sure I'm guilty of some length of time, but I often wonder what they are doing up there. A few guests have mentioned that they wash their clothes with them in the shower.

When guests arrive, I now discuss water conservation with them and that I am happy to help with any laundry services. If they still insist on long shower sessions, I leave the house so I can focus on other things and let it go.

The common area in the kitchen is where I've had to learn to let go the most, and I've gotten pretty easygoing with having the kitchen open twenty-four hours a day. At times, I've made a nice dinner, cleaned the dishes, and put the kitchen to bed only to have a guest come home at nine p.m. and cook a meal. Not only is there the aroma of the food, but also the banging and clattering of the pots and pans. Over the years, various pans and dishes have been broken, so I've learned to put certain types of items away that I don't want guests to use. Yes, in our home you'll find a couple Le Creuset pots and pans in the linen closet. It's a necessary step to protect some of my possessions I'm particularly fond of and careful about.

I have a glass-enclosed shelf in my kitchen which holds special glasses and serving items. It contains a decorative, handblown glass dish that I made on a trip to a glassblowing studio on Whidbey Island. I came home from work once and found it filled with a guest's leftovers in the fridge! Instead of making a big deal about it, I carefully transferred the items to a more appropriate bowl for leftovers and called it a day. Guess where that dish went for the remainder of their stay? You guessed it: the linen closet.

I once had a young woman stay for several months over the summer. She was sweet and we enjoyed hosting her. She stayed in the room with the shared bath. It was a good thing I had my eyes on the bathroom each day. After the first couple of weeks, I noticed a tremendous amount of her hair on the floor and in the tub. I mentioned to her that since it was a shared space if she could clean the hair off the drain, then the tub would remain decent for the next person.

I didn't notice an improvement. She typically showered in the evening, so after every shower I would go in and remove the hair from the drain and tub. I'm not sure why she didn't take ownership of her mess in a shared space, but I was adamant that the tub remain clean for anyone using the bathroom. If she was not going to clean up after herself, then I would. It was my home after all. It did prove to be a bit frustrating, but since that seemed to be her only vice in an otherwise great personality, I figured it was a battle not worth fighting.

As I've mentioned, I do occasionally enjoy cooking a meal or treat to share with a guest, mainly breakfast items like bread, scones, or a fruit salad. The funniest story happened when a guest left me a note during their stay, thanking me for the banana bread. There was banana bread on the counter, but I had intended to package it as gifts for friends, not necessarily for the guests. Apparently, my guest found it first. I'm glad they enjoyed it! I shrugged it off and moved on.

It's more common than I like for people to help themselves to condiments and milk in the fridge. This is not a customary practice, nor should a guest assume that any food in the host's fridge is fair game. Again, I don't mind sharing if someone asks. However, when people don't ask, then I shake my head and ask myself what is worth focusing on and if it's better to address the situation on my own and move forward. I'll only work myself up if I hold onto any anxiety or frustration, which isn't healthy for me or any other host.

<u>**Key Points to Remember**</u>

- Have a home maintenance schedule for repairs and seasonal work around the home, and any emergency repair numbers readily available.

- You'll go crazy seeking perfection in the home. Do your best to maintain a clean and safe environment but don't sweat every detail. I remind myself that our guests know that we live here, too, and in general, will try to be considerate.

- Pick your battles as to what's most important to ask a guest to do and what you can willingly *do* for the guest. Remember the focus is to keep your guests happy.

- Sometimes getting it done and moving forward is more important than making it perfect!

Chapter 5

Cleaning and Washing

Some of you may agree that your washer and dryer are among the best modern conveniences. On a typical weekend, I might have to do five loads of laundry. That's a lot of clothes, bed linens, and towels. As you may have guessed, it's not just the washing—that's the easy part. It's the remaking of the beds and folding the clothes that's so time consuming.

One service I provide is if guests stay with me longer than one week, then laundry services are included. Meaning: I do the laundry. Guests will often comment that they are happy to do their own laundry, but I cheerfully smile and tell them firmly I'll take care of it for them. This truly is my one non-negotiable, and I'm not ready to let it go.

The reason is that if a guest uses the washer or dryer and they break, then I can't turn the rooms on time. It's up to me to make this all happen in a short amount of time, and some days, it's a well-orchestrated machine. This is my preference, and you might opt to allow guests to do their own laundry.

Doing guests' laundry can be quite time-consuming, but I feel it's necessary to make sure that the machines stay in operating order. I can't even imagine having to flip a room while sitting at a laundromat feeding quarters into the machine all afternoon. It would be an inconvenience and an expense to get the appliances fixed, and therefore, cut into my profits.

When the guests arrive home from their day, their clothes are washed and folded on their bed. I think about how lucky those summer interns were since they didn't have to do their own laundry for the entire summer. And why not? They were visiting the area and should have been out enjoying Seattle on the weekends. Every month, I get a notice from Puget Sound Energy showing my consumption of gas and electricity in relation to my neighbors. Mine is always much higher, but it's worth it!

Several years ago, I had the opportunity to stay with a wonderful couple in Portland, Oregon, who were friendly and hospitable. Their home was wonderful and in a nice, quiet neighborhood. The gardens off their main room looked like pages out of *Better Homes and Gardens*. I was pleased with my choice of accommodations.

My first evening there, however, I wasn't as thrilled. When I got into bed, the linens had an overwhelming scent of perfume or detergent. Trying to sleep when you can't breathe is a challenge! For that reason, I have become extra careful to not use heavily scented laundry soap and harsh chemical cleaning supplies. Many people have skin or olfactory sensitivities to strong chemicals, perfumes, and air fresheners. Six years ago, I switched to H_2O at Home cleaning products, which are produced in France. The cleaning products come with a chiffonnette scrubber and are effective and easy to use. It makes cleaning the house a delight since I'm not ingesting harsh chemicals, either. It's a win-win for me and the guest.

Keeping the home clean, fresh, and comfortable is an obvious priority. I work hard to stay clear of harsh chemicals or disinfectant sprays, but sometimes you need to pull out the Lysol spray! I had one guest kindly communicate with me while I was at work that he had burned something in the microwave because he had let the timer go for too long. He asked if it was okay to open a window. This happened in

January, so the weather was quite cold. I told him yes and thought that was that…until I got home.

I walked upstairs to discover a haze of smoke hovered on the ceiling in the kitchen. The burnt smell overwhelmed me as much as the lingering smoke. It seemed the window had not been left open long enough before he left for the day.

Originally, I did try the natural remedy for getting the smoke smell out of the microwave: vinegar with water and lemons with water, but to no avail. For the smoke and smell in the kitchen, I opened the sliding door and had to succumb to using Lysol spray. We couldn't use the microwave for a week or so in order for the smell to dissipate. It took us several days to get the smell out of my home.

While keeping my house fresh and clean, I've learned that food isn't the only problem that can smell. I also had an attorney who came to stay with us who was working in Seattle and needed a room for a week. When I opened the door to greet him, he smelled like a skunk!

I called my friend and said, "You won't believe this guy's smell. What do I do? It smells awful!"

She proceeded to educate me by stating the man had probably smoked pot. Again, I bought some Lysol and one of those Renuzit wicks to put in his room. He was so happy with his stay that he wanted to book again. I simply had to tell him that the room was not available. There are times when you need to consider the comfort of your family and other guests in the shared space.

So, how else do I keep the home smelling nice and fresh? Even though we live in Seattle, we do leave the windows to our upstairs bathrooms open a lot. This helps to circulate the air in the room and keeps the temperature at a consistent level as heat rises. And fresh air is good for the soul!

We occasionally run a diffuser by the front door on the weekends when I am home. A small diffuser with several drops of my favorite lemon essential oil smells nice and bright and is a good welcome when you walk in the home. On occasion, we burn candles, but I do that rarely because I don't want to encourage guests to burn candles in their room.

Lots of new information is available regarding certain houseplants being natural purifiers for the air in our homes. There's nothing a Seattle person wants more in their home during winter than some houseplants and color. I've tried adding more houseplants to the home and rooms, but someone inevitably knocks over the container without notifying me. I usually find potting soil on the desk or carpet where they let it sit. For that reason, the plants are limited in our home.

Key Points to Remember

- Establish your preferences and policies for long-term guests regarding laundry, cooking, or any other service. Will you provide the service or give them access to your laundry room, kitchen, etc.?

- Be aware of the reality that people have strong sensitivities to scent. Decide what type of air fresheners you'll use in the home and if you'll make any available for guests to use in their specific rooms.

Chapter 6

Is a Broken Elbow Worth It?

One summer day, I was upstairs in the master bedroom rushing to flip a room while my daughter was downstairs. I started to remake the bed with the freshly laundered sheets when I noticed a huge stain of some sort in two spots on the fabric headboard presumably left there by the previous guests.

Upon seeing this, I became extremely upset because we hadn't had many items that had been damaged at that point. A fabric headboard can be tricky to clean without leaving evidence of the stain. Thinking that I would continue to make the bed and then work at stain removal, I became increasingly upset and my movement back and forth around the bed became quick and sharp. Suddenly, the bottom of my tennis shoe caught on the carpet, and I went straight down on the ground with arms extended to stop my fall. Searing pain shot through my arms, and I cried out. My daughter happened to be home and came rushing to my rescue.

She and I determined that, based on the pain in my wrists, it was best to go to the urgent care. Several hours later, the doctor said I had broken my right elbow—simply because I let the anger take over, got in my head, and lost my footing. Fortunately, my other arm was fine, but it wasn't my dominant arm. Either way, the verdict was grim.

For weeks I had my arm in a wrap or sling to help with the healing, which made hosting and cleaning a serious challenge. Fortunately, no cast was required, but I faced a bigger issue. How was I going to flip rooms when I had an immobile arm? Coincidentally, I had taken on a commitment to help another Airbnb family in Seattle flip their home and cottage so that they could spend the summer in Europe.

There was no way I was going to email them and let them know that I was unable to help with the management of their home. So, I solicited the help of my daughter and best friend to help me flip the Seattle home more than once prior to their return, which was burdensome and painful, but I felt so grateful for the assistance of friends and family.

This became a critical lesson for me. Is frustration worth your health? For me, this one scenario compromised my physical and mental health. Not only did it impact my ability to manage my own home and my friend's Seattle home, but I had a difficult time getting around in my full-time job. I needed both my mom and son to drive me around during the day to see clients. Now when I see something frustrating, I stop and pull myself together and manage to ask myself if it's really worth it before charging ahead full speed.

You might be wondering if I got the stain out of the fabric headboard. I did get the stain out, but it left an even larger water stain on the headboard. Since that time, another stain has appeared as well. When we furnished the second room with a headboard and dresser, I kept in mind that the items needed to be tasteful and in good condition, but if it was damaged, I wouldn't be upset because nothing is worth a broken elbow.

I've had other items in my house damaged as well. I purchased a friend's aunt's antique desk, thinking it would go well in the new bedroom we were designing. It does look beautiful, and I've taken good care of it and provided guests with coasters to protect it. Recently, I saw that a guest had put her beauty products and hair gel on top of the desk, leaving rings and even some residue from the product as it dried and stuck to the desk. There was another desk that could have been used in the room, but unfortunately, the antique desk bore the brunt of her use.

While remaining calm, I did work at getting the residue off the desk, but it was permanently damaged. My friend had entrusted me with this desk, and I felt a responsibility to keep it in good shape. I have plans to install a custom glass top that will protect any future mishaps.

Recently, I was doing some light cleaning for an extended guest. That meant I would also be emptying trash, dusting, and vacuuming in their room. I noticed that the lamp was on the floor with a broken light bulb shattered all over the carpet. How long had he been occupying the room with the shattered light bulb on the floor? It could've started a fire, or he could've been hurt stepping on the glass. Getting in and out of bed could be dangerous with those broken fragments. Obviously, I cleaned the mess, but I did send him a note through the Airbnb site that I had cleaned up the mess and replaced the light bulb and to please let me know in the future if an item gets broken so I can fix it.

One gentleman stayed with us for several months as a summer intern. He would use his bike for commuting. When he first arrived, I told him that it was fine for him to come in and out of the garage to store the bike. Instead of using the electric garage door opener as I suggested, he manually pulled up the garage door and jammed the track. I was able to get it fixed but shook my head regarding his forgetfulness of how to operate the garage door.

During another long-term guest visit, I went into the bathroom to do some cleaning, tidy the room, and empty the trash cans. When I went to clean the shower, I noticed lots of tiny black specs all over the shower. Examining them further offered no explanation. What were these tiny black flecks, and how was I going to get them off?

Later, I noticed a box of black hair dye in the trash. It took me several hours to get each and every one of those pieces of black dye off the shower walls by using my fingernail to scrape each and every spec since they didn't remove with my other tools. I did have to mention to him that future hair-dyeing sessions were out of the question.

Airbnb does provide their hosts a million-dollar insurance policy in case an item or the home is damaged. However, most of the incidences we've had would be considered minor, and in my opinion, would not qualify for a claim submission. Also, I'm not sure if submitting a claim affects my standings and visibility on the site. I've never wanted to test it, so I haven't submitted a claim since nothing major has ever been damaged. I did catch that stovetop fire in time!

It is frustrating that people do not treat their guest property like they would their own home. Or do they? When I've stayed at others' homes, I've taught my kids to leave the home/condo/room better than they found it. We always strip the beds, clean the bathroom, and sometimes vacuum the place before we leave, especially when we stay at a place on the beach. I want my hosts to know that I appreciated and respected their place and would like to stay with them again. My hope is that other people will do the same.

<u>Key Points to Remember</u>

- Don't leave any valuable or memorable furniture or accessories in an accessible place where they can be ruined or broken. If it's valuable, then lock it away.

- Don't let your frustration regarding a guest and their behavior wear down your mental health, even for a few moments. Learn from my hard lesson of the broken elbow. Haste in anger only causes more problems.

- Have a back-up plan in case of a personal emergency where you cannot maintain your property.

Chapter 7

Life Isn't Always Fair

Haven't we repeatedly heard from our parents that life isn't always fair? The saying is almost like an automatic loop that plays over and over again. I've often felt that life should be fair, and we should each get a chance to express our opinions in a difficult situation. I have had a couple of instances where I've needed to rally for myself and reach out to make sure that my feelings about a situation were expressed and the right thing, in my opinion, was done.

A recent case happened when I had a guest reach out to me to book a room for a two-month stay over the summer. The guest and I began having a conversation as she asked questions about my home. The guest stated that she and her husband loved being outdoors and wondered if I had a nice backyard, where the home was located, and was it quiet?

I responded back that yes, we did have a nice backyard that was fairly private, and that I maintained a lovely garden in the summer and took a lot of pride in providing guests the option to sit outside and enjoy the backyard. I even mentioned that she could access the Wi-Fi from the backyard in case she wanted to work. I encouraged her to read the reviews on the site as a lot of past guests had commented on different aspects of the home and its comfort level.

After some time of communication and reading her past reviews as a guest, I pre-approved her. Once the pre-approval was finished, this individual replied, "I'm not obligated to tell you, but I have an emotional support dog that travels with me. I see that you too have a dog, and I wanted to be sure that it's okay to bring my dog."

Immediately, I politely commented back to this person, saying that in the description of the home it clearly states that we already have a dog and that the home is not suitable for other pets. We had some additional dialogue, and I told her that perhaps this was not a good fit since our dog is elderly and protective of her space. In other words, this rental is a shared space.

The next day, I got an email from Airbnb reminding me of their non-discrimination policy, and that I was not allowed to refuse this individual the opportunity to stay in my home because of her emotional support animal. They also flagged my profile, which meant that I was a concern to them based on this incident. This woman had taken it upon herself to reach out to Airbnb after our conversation and complain that she was being discriminated against because I would not allow her to stay in my home with her dog.

You cannot imagine how upset this email made me. I have always been generous of my space to other guests. We offer people an experience in a home which is our primary residence, sometimes with more than one guest at a time. My ultimate goal is making sure that everyone, including my dog, is safe and comfortable in our home.

After receiving Airbnb's email, I called Airbnb's customer service to express my concern over the email. I wanted to have a conversation with an actual human to try to resolve the issue by making sure that they understood the situation in the home. I called, and was immediately connected to an associate who took the time to listen to my recap of the events and explain why we couldn't allow an additional pet in the home.

After a couple of days of emailing back-and-forth with Airbnb, it was determined that my home profile would have a note on it that guest animals would not be permitted in the home due to the circumstances with our dog and because we offered a shared space with other guests. Our home is not suitable for other pets. Period.

I understand that some people do need the support of an emotional support animal, and I'm happy to know that there are different options of pets to suit different needs, but every hosts' home may not be conducive to hosting another pet, which I had stated in my home profile already. I believe that potential guests should be sensitive to the fact that they are choosing to stay in someone's personal residence if they don't choose a private rental option.

There are other listings in the area which do accommodate animals that she could have easily inquired about, but she felt that she needed to own the situation by calling Airbnb and filing a report.

So, why didn't I simply withdraw her pre-approval? Airbnb classifies some hosts as Superhosts. A Superhost meets the following requirements: responds within a twenty-four-hour time period to a reservation request, has superior reviews, and doesn't cancel on a guest. If I had cancelled her reservation once she mentioned the dog, I would have lost my Superhost status.

What does a Superhost status provide, and why is it so important? On the Airbnb site, Superhosts are highlighted with a badge on their profile picture which reassures visitors that the host they are booking with is a high-quality host. The potential guest can rest assured after seeing that badge and reading the reviews that they will more than likely have a good experience.

In the end, I'm sure this individual found a nice place to stay that was better suited for her and her pet, rather than having an unhappy experience with us for several months. I appreciate that Airbnb took the time to understand my concerns and hers regarding an emotional support dog. Airbnb takes their policies seriously, and I appreciate this level of commitment to the guest and host.

On another note, Airbnb recently removed the requirement to have users provide a profile picture. I had heard there were hosts who were making pre-determinations about a guest based on how they looked. A host can still ask for a picture since it's nice to know that the person who made the reservation is the person who is actually arriving at your door and staying in the guest accommodations. The current procedure as of 2020 is that the host must state in the house rules that a profile picture must be provided after a reservation has been accepted. You must also state this in your home description as well.

Another opportunity where I felt that I needed to call Airbnb and make things right is when I was unfairly reviewed by a guest. Remember the lady and her son who stayed in my home and accidentally lit a fire on the ceramic stovetop? They were unfamiliar with working appliances, and we had a language barrier. I later found out that when they checked out, they wrote a derogatory review in their native language.

I copied their comments into a translator, and I was floored by what I read! They said things concerning me and my home that were completely untrue. I could not figure out why they would have done that. Despite their challenges in our home, I was extremely patient with them and took a lot of time to chat with the woman's son to get to know him and ask about his camp over the summer weeks.

When a review is submitted by a guest, you have the opportunity to respond publicly to their comment. First, I contacted Airbnb to discuss the situation with them and ask what could be done regarding this review. Reviews are essential for both the guest and the host. If a host receives a bad review, their rating goes down and other potential guests read it and take it into consideration prior to booking the property.

On the flip side, I never skip reading the reviews of guests who reach out to book a room. I want to know about a person who may stay in our home and have sometimes declined requests based on their poor reviews.

My conversation with the associate at Airbnb went well. They considered my past reviews and my standing with Airbnb. When I wrote my review of this couple in the private notes to Airbnb, I noted that these people were not suited to the home-sharing platform. They would be better suited at a hotel, considering the issues that arose during their stay. In the end, Airbnb removed the review from my profile, which I felt was fair.

Those were the only two times that I have gone to Airbnb and asked them to take the time to review a situation and hear my side of the story. They were helpful, and I feel both instances were resolved well. Life may not always be fair, but we should be treated fairly.

Key Points to Remember

- As a host you will be thrown some curve balls! Take a deep breath and proceed with caution and enthusiasm. We can only grow from the opportunities we face.

- If you feel that you've been unfairly treated by a guest, it's fine to reach out to Airbnb directly to resolve an issue. Despite what some people say, Airbnb is there to support the hosting community, resolve issues, and listen to hosts. Without us, their guests have to book with a hotel, so it's in their best interest to work well with hosts, too.

- Make the call to Airbnb immediately. Don't sit on the situation for days or weeks deciding what to do. The longer you wait, the longer it will take to get the situation resolved in a satisfactory manner.

Chapter 8

Appreciation

Throughout this book, I have mentioned several instances when I've been appreciative of the opportunities we've had as a family thanks to our Airbnb experiences. When we stay as guests, we like to bring a little treasure from Seattle to leave with our host or leave a handwritten thank you note to show appreciation for sharing their space with us.

I provide a personalized note on our guests' beds with a delicious chocolate when they arrive at our home. Needless to say, it's usually locally sourced chocolate like Theo or Seattle Chocolate. Most guests love a touch of something from the area and think it's thoughtful. My friend and fellow host, Patty, leaves a bottle of local wine for her extended visitors. It's a beautiful token, and I know people are surprised and appreciative of their host's efforts.

We had a pleasant guest from Paris stay with us. He worked at the local L'Oréal site in Redmond for a week. We had a fun time getting to know him and his business. When he left, I came home to a thank you note and a dozen red roses in a vase. What a kind gesture!

One of my guests from Mexico City brought some brilliantly colored placemats and coasters to leave as a thank you for her time with us. How thoughtful that she had taken the time to bring an unusual gift that had special meaning from her own city.

Another couple from Hawaii came to visit in the summer for a seminar. Any free time they had was spent sourcing locally grown items in the area. Seeking out anything fresh and local was a treat, as most foods are shipped to the islands. One day, I came home to local fruit and flowers picked from a nearby farm. I was touched they had thought of me during their stay.

Several other guests have left either a handwritten thank you note, a bottle of wine, fresh flowers from the farmers' market, or even a Chick-fil-A gift card. The givers of the gift card were shocked that I had never tried the food at Chick-fil-A and insisted that I needed to get there soon.

Recently, I had a North Dakota student stay with me for a couple of months during her internship. She was a delightful guest, and we enjoyed getting to know her and giving her tips on places to see around the Puget Sound. During her stay, her family came out for a brief visit, and they toured the area together. On their way out of town, I met them briefly and had a great conversation.

Several weeks later, my son and I received an unexpected card from her parents explaining how grateful their daughter was that she enjoyed her independent travel without feeling alone. They thanked us for providing her a safe, charming home and for welcoming her with such warmth. In all the years that we've hosted interns, we've never received a note of appreciation from a parent. The student had been every bit as thoughtful and nice as her mother, who had written the considerate card. I keep the card as a reminder of great times when the going gets rough.

One guest stayed with us for a weekend to participate in an event as a vendor at our local state park. The event sounded amazing, and she offered me two free tickets for that Saturday. The tickets were valued at two hundred dollars apiece! I was touched she would consider giving me a couple of the free tickets she was allocated. These gifts are never expected and don't come often, but when they do it's a sweet surprise and a good reminder for me to be thoughtful of my hosts when I'm a guest.

<u>Key Points to Remember</u>

- When you become a host, I strongly recommend you think of a small, thoughtful token you can leave in your guests' rooms or kitchen.

- Not every host does something, and it's certainly not expected, but it will make you stand out from other hosts who do nothing. It can be a treat or a treasure unique to your area or even a handwritten note that shows you've taken the extra time to welcome the guest.

- Be gracious of the gifts brought to you, even if they aren't your style or taste. The guests are trying to extend a kindness in return for their stay. They typically aren't thoughtful if they did not enjoy their stay.

Chapter 9

Friendship

I have been fortunate to have some amazing friends and family in my life, and they've all been wonderfully supportive of my Airbnb adventures. Some, in the beginning, thought I was crazy for letting complete strangers stay in my home. Having been a regular Airbnb and bed-and-breakfast guest already, I didn't feel it was all that foreign of an idea to share my home.

I've taken many walks with friends, and they've either asked or I've offered the latest tale or conundrum with a current guest. There were many times that I needed to vent. Sometimes they would laugh, but oftentimes they would look at me in disbelief. When something outrageous happened or an event like the emotional support dog occurred, my family, a friend, or both, are who I call to use as a sounding board. I would ask them "Am I crazy or…?" I can tell you that my friends and family have been great listeners to my stories, and we've had many laughs over the years!

When I first created a profile with pictures of our home, I reached out to another host in the area who lives close by but has a different type of space in her home. Barbara lives a mile from me and had turned her entire downstairs into a private suite with a bath, bedroom, sitting room, and mini kitchen. She generously shared her time and gave me tips and guidance for various situations that could arise. I wouldn't have been as successful in this venture had it not been for her. She has become a friend, and we continue to support each other and help each other when one of us goes on vacation or needs to have a local contact for a guest if an issue arises.

The hosts in the Airbnb community are supportive of one another and many friendships are formed. I've paid this forward as some of my friends have expressed an interest in getting started on the home-sharing platform.

To date, I've helped four friends through the process of launching their profiles, answering questions, and helping in those moments when they, too, needed some advice during a tricky or difficult situation with a guest. Since it's a new experience, the Airbnb platform can be a bit confusing when you're learning the ropes and working within the website can be daunting. It's nice to have a mentor when you start out, someone who can guide you through the various do's and don'ts, like I did. I'm happy to say their listings are successful, and three of them continue to host today. It's great to see how the revenue from those listing has been used to enrich their lives.

It's also been fun to establish friendships with some of my guests as well. Oftentimes, you'll have a guest with whom you hit it off. We've had quite a few of them in our home. Some are repeat guests who are here for business, and some stay once, and we never see them again.

We have one mother/daughter duo who have stayed with us repeatedly over the years. They are from out of the country but have family here in the area, so their trips occur once or twice a year. The first time I met them, the mother was battling health issues. They notified me ahead of her visit, so I made sure to personally welcome her to the home.

When I first opened the door, she looked like her life was on the line; she was frail, pale, and tired after the long flight. We made her as comfortable as we could while she stayed with us for her treatments. This happened several more times, and we were so thrilled to see her progress successfully.

One day, I received an email from her that they had an alarming situation with her health while they were traveling, and asked if they could possibly fly into Seattle and stay with us. Immediately, I panicked. I had another guest in her usual room but our second room with the shared bath was vacant. I needed to ask the current guest if she wouldn't mind moving into the other room with the shared bath so that the mother and daughter could have the room with the bath.

I was petrified as I went to ask the current guest and worried she would be inconvenienced. At the same time, I felt I was doing the right thing. I told her that I wouldn't charge her for the weekend if she agreed to make the accommodation. She was happy to switch and all was well. I reimbursed her through the site and when she checked out, she left cash equaling one night's stay on the table. That was so thoughtful of her!

This was the only time I have ever asked a guest to unexpectedly shift their living arrangements, but again, I felt I was doing it for someone who had become a friend and was more than a guest. I'm happy to report that she is doing well, and I'll be seeing her again in a couple of months for a return visit.

We had another couple who got married, sold their worldly possessions, and moved out to the beautiful Pacific Northwest. Danny was making a career move, and Casey was studying for a pharmacy exam. They were not ready to put down roots, so they were staying in different Airbnb locations until Casey had passed his exam and got a permanent position, which would determine their final destination. They stayed with us off and on for several weeks.

They were so much fun, and we loved having them in our home. They've been busy with their relocation and getting accustomed to their new city, which is one-and-a-half hours away from us. We still get together on occasion to have dinner and share stories and adventures. They are a delightful couple, and we feel so blessed to have met them through this experience.

During a recent summer we had an intern booked for a month. Her arrival night coincided with my supper club event. The house was full and a bit noisy, so I invited her to come and participate, meet my friends, and have some great food. This worked out perfectly when she arrived thirty minutes before my friends did and was able to unpack and come down to join us. We got to know her better, and it helped her feel more comfortable during her stay. She even reached out on her own to several of the people from the supper club to do activities one-on-one.

I have another guest who lives in Washington but comes to my area frequently. She stays a couple of evenings a couple times a year, but we are often found together at the breakfast counter catching up on each other's lives and having a good time. We don't communicate outside of the visits but when she does come back, it's a fun reunion.

Business travelers can be consistent, too, and we do build a relationship with many of them. With our home being so close to Microsoft, Google, and other tech companies, we often get contractors, workers, and interns. We also have young people who come for several weeks to attend a summer camp, and their mothers will accompany them on the trip. It's fun to be able to give them suggestions for things to do and see while their child is at the camp. I've made friendships with a lot of these women, and we've had some fun visits. I'm usually sorry to see them go and think if they lived nearby, we would be fast friends.

By allowing your space to become a home for

guests, you open yourself to a vast array of potential friendships. This has been one of the most rewarding aspects of the job. It's your choice as the host as to who you want to befriend and how close you want to invite them into your inner circle. By cracking the door open, you'll reap the rewards.

Key Points to Remember

- Open yourself to the possibility of making lifelong friends through sharing your space!

- People are longing for connection in this increasingly disconnected world. By traveling with Airbnb, they are seeking a unique experience. The personal connections with their hosts can provide those intimate one-of-a-kind encounters.

- Don't stress that every person will become a friend until you're overwhelmed with friends. Some guests are friends that you talk with only when they come to stay. Others may never become friends. Keep the option open for those who are longing to have *you* be their friend.

Chapter 10

Advice from Other Airbnb Hosts

If you would like to become a host but you are intimidated by the idea of sharing your personal space, I understand. It's a common concern that people express to me frequently. I thought it would be helpful to include some experiences from my friends, Donna and Patty, who have become Airbnb hosts after watching my adventure unfold. They each host differently than I do, but also find it rewarding. You may appreciate their stories because their host experiences are quite different from mine.

Donna has a downstairs suite with a separate entrance, and Patty has a listing for an entire home located east of the mountains. Both listings are different than mine because they interact with their guests through the Airbnb site, but they don't share a common space.

Donna's suite has its own entrance for her guests that is separate from the main home. She appreciates being able to offer a private experience for guests who prefer to have their own space and are not entirely comfortable with sharing common living areas. They receive the comfort of home without feeling like they're intruding on a family. This allows privacy for her own family, and she's not obligated to have conversations with strangers. The arrangement works great if you want to host, don't own another property, and lean more towards being an introvert who needs your space.

The separate area creates some interesting situations, though. On one occasion, the power went out, and she felt terrible because the guest didn't have a way to make coffee. Donna heated a thermos of boiling water using her gas stovetop and delivered it to them. I'm sure it was a bit of a hassle for Donna, but she felt it was her responsibility to make her guests as comfortable as possible, which is what creates the perfect Airbnb experience. We can't always control the situations for our guests, but we can make the best out of a difficult situation.

Her most memorable guests were two gentlemen who were getting their graduate degrees in physical therapy. They stayed with her while they were working a ten-week rotation in a nearby city. These men were organized and would do their laundry and food prep upstairs every Sunday with Donna. They would prepare all their meals ahead for the week and store them in Ziploc bags. She was impressed with their meal prep skills as they worked within the house rules that afforded them one day per week to use the full upstairs kitchen, rather than their mini one.

Her most stressful guest was one who ventured down the blame game road. One morning, Donna had to leave early. Her guest said that even though the posted quiet hours lasted until six a.m., he was awakened at 5:45 a.m. by her departure, which meant the hosts broke their own rules. Later, he blamed their son, who was visiting from college, for waking him as the son moved furniture around.

I asked Donna how she would handle a guest like this in the future, and she had the perfect answer. "We have to take the high road by thanking them for staying with us and avoiding point-by-point rebuttals. There will always be argumentative people out there, and my mission in life does not include changing those personality types."

Just remember: you can't change people.

Donna offered these tips for hosting people in an adjoining property like hers:

- Every guest is different. Some people will want to meet the host and others don't care. Try to gauge your guest's interest level for face-to-face interactions as you communicate with them prior to their arrival.
- Ease of guest check-in is a top priority. This means providing clear instructions, excellent lighting, and entrance-access pictures if possible. Make sure to answer the phone if they try to call you!
- Milk and cookies are nice. You don't need to go overboard with expensive wine and chocolates. Another nice touch is to put half-and-half or unflavored creamer in the fridge for morning coffee.
- Stock extra toilet paper in obvious locations for guests to find.
- Put a toilet plunger by the toilet. No one wants to call a host and tell them the toilet is clogged.
- Don't be surprised if guests choose to remove their trash and put it in your trash bin upon checkout. That's part of the guests' booking for a private space. Make this easy for guests by providing easy access to the trash and recycling bins.
- If the power or internet goes out, check on your guests immediately and let them know you are aware of the situation and how soon you think it will be resolved.
- As part of the turnaround during cleaning after checkout, make sure the TVs are working normally. Some guests may change the input cables to plug in their own devices.

- Provide a fan and a space heater. You never know what temperature a guest prefers, and it may be quite different from your own preferences.
- Be open to listening to any guests' suggestions. Guests know best!

* * *

Patty's second home is in a beautiful location, but her challenge is that she can never meet guests upon arrival and can't respond in person when a problematic situation arises, due to the distance between her residence and her rental house. This can cause some worry for her during each guest's stay. However, what she likes best about having an off-site listing is guests can stay in her favorite spot in the world due to its secluded location which is nestled in the woods east of Seattle. She hopes they enjoy the home as much as she does when she stays there.

Patty has had many memorable guests. One person put a new toilet seat on the toilet and never mentioned it to her. Since the rental is some distance from her own home, she uses a cleaning service to help flip the rooms, so she's not sure when the update occurred. She'd like to take this opportunity to thank whomever they may be!

On the flip side, she had a family who left dirty diapers in the indoor trashcans that stunk up the entire house long before the cleaners could come in and do a complete cleaning. Ugh! Thankfully, the housekeepers handled the situation professionally and made the house fresh and clean in time for the next guests. Another family's children jumped on the beds and yanked down the curtains, tearing them in the process, which then needed to be replaced.

Patty's most tricky guest was a person who insisted he would be fine staying at her home in the midst of an enormous wildfire with Level 3 evacuations happening. All the roads and highways were closed, and he kept saying, "Oh, I'll make it somehow." The guest would not accept the fact that she needed to cancel his stay for safety reasons. He insisted on moving forward and putting his own life on the line by trying to reach an area that was being evacuated.

In cases of dangerous situations like wildfire or other natural disasters, Airbnb will grace the host with a cancellation since the situation is out of their control and the safety of the guest is the first priority.

Patty offered a few tips for people who offer off-site vacation homes:

- Install locks on a few of your closets and/or garage so that you can keep your own items there.
- Have a professional and reliable cleaning service who can handle minor repairs, pick up supplies, and respond to guest requests in a timely manner. Pay them what they are worth!
- Write a heartfelt letter, along with house instructions, so guests can care for your place as you would. This should include info for how to operate the stove, microwave, breaker box, thermostat, Wi-Fi, TV, and any house rules you expect them to follow. (Patty's never had a major problem and feels that it's because of her detailed welcome letter.)
- Install an easy-to-use lockbox for the key and hang a small flashlight right next to it for those who are checking in late in the evening. Make sure your cleaning crew checks the batteries occasionally.

<u>Key Points to Remember</u>

-   Home sharing comes in many forms, and
    you don't need to limit yourself to sharing
    space inside your current home. Perhaps
    you have a mother-in-law suite available
    that could generate some additional income.
    I've seen lots of creative possibilities on the
    Airbnb website, including Airstream trailers
    and boats available for rent, sometimes
    parked in the host's yard.

-   There are many ways to accomplish a task.
    Don't let another host tell you that their way
    is the only way to host. Take each guests'
    input and create your own unique experience
    for your guest. They stayed in your place for
    a reason and can provide invaluable insight
    on what to improve for the next guest. It's
    important to be proactive, too.

Chapter 11

Mother Nature and Guest Safety

Living in the Pacific Northwest, we have our fair share of wind, rain, and even snow. We can't control the weather, and it can cause stress for guests who are arriving and departing our neighborhood.

It's common for a storm to knock out power to our house while we have guests staying there. We keep a nice, big, portable battery-operated lamp on their dresser, so they have emergency lighting even if I'm not home. On rare occasions, a guest is scheduled to arrive while we've been without power for over twenty-four hours. This prompts the thought process: do I need to reach out and cancel, or how long do I wait before I notify them that power has been out and may not be on when they arrive? It's a matter of chance, and I'm happy to say that although losing power has been an inconvenience, we have never had to cancel on a guest.

It's a well-known fact that Seattle gets a lot of rain. I guess we do, but it's only a constant drizzle. We often have guests who come unprepared for the rain and don't have the right gear. I had one guest who thought going to a Seahawks game during his stay would be fun. When he prepared to leave for the game, I saw what he was (or wasn't) wearing and told him we couldn't let him go without some clothing to help keep him warm and dry. Luckily, my son and he were similar sizes, and my son had a nice rain jacket and scarf for the guest to use.

Later, he expressed appreciation that we noticed his lack of proper clothing because he would have had a miserable time at the wet and cold game that day.

We have a bin of umbrellas that are available to guests since a lot of our guests walk or use public transportation. They certainly shouldn't wait for the bus in the pouring rain without an umbrella or jacket to keep them dry.

We also get snow, and 2019 was a tremendous year for snow and ice. Generally, we only get a couple of inches of snow but what the rest of the country doesn't realize is that the Seattle area isn't equipped with enough snowplows to de-ice and plow all the streets in a timely fashion. This results in a lasting layer of snow and ice, and if you've visited Seattle, you know we have lots of hills. Hills plus snow and ice make for great car sledding!

This banner snow year left around two feet of snow in our area making it extremely dangerous to get in and out of the neighborhood. Good communication with the arriving guests meant that I needed to let them know to rent a front-wheel drive or four-wheel drive vehicle so they could navigate the hill to our house safely. A local resident chose to stay with us so she could be closer to work during that week to avoid a long commute in the snow. Even her vehicle got stuck at the bottom of the hill, and she couldn't make it to the top.

Our front steps to the home can also get packed with snow and ice during these times, so I have people arrive and depart the home through the garage. Not the most glamourous entry, but it is the safest to avoid slipping on ice. As a host, I have to make sure that guests have safe arrivals and departures.

On one snowy evening, I made a delicious pot of homemade chili and cornbread and told our two guests to help themselves. I usually don't make a meal like this and offer it to guests, but the stores were low on food and having a stash of food wasn't my guests' highest priority. A homemade meal when they got back to the house was probably welcomed. There were also endless amounts of homemade cookies and biscotti. What's a girl to do when it's snowing? The guests definitely scored on the baked goods that winter!

<u>Key Points to Remember</u>
- Be mindful of weather conditions and how they affect guests' safety. Clear and prompt communication is key to help guests navigate and access the home in severe weather.

- Think ahead about providing emergency lighting and heating and have these items in obvious places for guests to find.

- Treat your guests like family. Don't let them go out in the cold or rain unprepared.

- Airbnb will let you cancel on a guest without penalty if there are extreme weather conditions that would jeopardize their safety in getting to your rental. Guest safety is paramount in all situations. My advice is that if you are concerned about the situation, then reach out to Airbnb and advise them of the situation. No doubt they have also received telephone calls from other hosts in the area, too.

Chapter 12

Human Nature

When you have multiple guests staying in the home at the same time and see two different types of personalities shine through, it can be interesting to observe how people react to varied situations. Here are some examples.

For two weeks, I had a man and woman stay with me in both bedrooms as separate renters. The gentleman was in his early sixties, and this was his first Airbnb experience. The young woman was just starting her career at Microsoft and was in her late twenties. I'll call them Jeff and Kate. Before the two guests came, I knew that I would be having a new double oven installed during their stay and forewarned them of which day to expect some noise and commotion.

Kate went off to work for her first day, and Jeff stayed in the home. No issues. When the installers came, they needed to cut a larger hole in the wall to accommodate the oven. I knew this would be happening and had been prepared. What we were not prepared for was the mess that the contractor created because he didn't tarp off the work area. Dust and debris flew all over the place. I was upset that the contractors weren't more careful during the installation and left it for me to clean.

It wasn't two minutes after the installers left that Jeff came down to the kitchen and wanted to make his lunch since it had been a few hours since breakfast. Obviously, I was a bit out of sorts as I started the process of cleaning, dusting, vacuuming, and mopping the entire first level of the house. In a polite but direct way, I told him that now wasn't a good time to fix a meal as the contractors had left a mess and the kitchen would need to be cleaned thoroughly before any meal preparation. He seemed quite put off by my explanation.

During the installation of the double oven, the microwave had to be removed. A new one had been ordered and would be picked up the next day. That evening, I offered to cook both Jeff and Kate's frozen dinners on the stovetop because I didn't want the first meal in the oven to be a frozen dinner. Kate was relaxed during the situation, but I could tell that Jeff wasn't amused. When the microwave finally arrived, Kate helped bring it in and install it. My son was there to help as well, but I was appreciative that she offered to help.

One peculiar instance during their stay happened when I noticed a broken glass on the counter one morning. I felt disappointed because the glass was unique, and I didn't know if I could find a replacement. Then, I noticed another part of the broken glass on the other counter. I thought little more about it and threw it away.

When I came home that morning from swimming with friends and was putting away groceries, I noticed glass on the floor. *You've got to be kidding! Who breaks a glass and doesn't pick up the pieces? Anyone could have stepped on it!*

I know who had drunk from the glass since I saw that person prior to heading down to my room for the evening. What's really crazy is when I saw him later that afternoon, he didn't even mention or apologize for breaking the glass. But he did want to know if I found his missing sock from the laundry I had washed two days ago. I found the sock and gave it to him. There was no mention at all to offer to replace the glass. The glass wasn't valuable, but the principle of missing apologies bothers me.

Three days later, the guest finally mentioned he'd broken the glass and offered to purchase a replacement. Unfortunately, I had already searched and could not find the same style.

I remind all my guests to turn off the lights when they leave an area to conserve electricity. I noticed that Jeff rarely, if ever, turned off lights wherever he went, which meant the lights ran all day while I was away at work. On the other hand, I would walk in the kitchen and see that the lights were off while Kate cooked her breakfast. I'd ask her if she wanted me to turn on the lights so she could see, and she'd say that she could see fine. The differences in the two guests' behaviors baffled me.

During those two weeks, Jeff lost his key. Fortunately, I don't put the house address on the key since I've had people lose the key before. He hardly left the house, so I don't know how he'd misplaced the key. He offered to replace the key, but since he didn't have a car it would have been a bigger hassle to find transportation to get him to the hardware store. It was easy enough to do it myself.

Remember how I sometimes lay bananas out on the counter so I can make some banana bread? Guess who threw them out in the garbage? And guess who missed out on some homemade banana bread?

If the dishwasher was running while either of them fixed a meal, Jeff would leave his dishes in the sink, but Kate would wash her dishes and put them away—never once put them in the dishwasher. The differences in the little things each guest did or didn't do fascinated me. As a host, you'll see a lot of these instances.

On the day before Jeff checked out of his room to head home, he came to me and said, "Tomorrow I'll be checking out."

"Yep, I have it on the calendar," I replied with a wink.

He continued, "I'm going to my class, and I'll be home around one p.m. to fix lunch and hang out for a bit, if that's okay?"

"Well, to be honest, I have a guest coming in tomorrow afternoon, so I will need to clean your room and shared bathroom," I countered. "You are welcome to pack up your belongings and put them by the door to pick up after your class."

"That sounds good. I'll come back, make my lunch, and hang out for a while until I leave," he said nonchalantly.

I looked at him and said, "Please keep in mind that checkout is at noon."

A seasoned traveler would have noted: pack bags, go to class, come back, pick up bags and leave. However, Jeff decided to come back at one p.m.— after checkout—fix his lunch and then hang out in the living room while I was upstairs cleaning and flipping his room. He had definitely overstayed his welcome!

When it came time to review his stay on the Airbnb website, I had a difficult time. I never like to say anything bad about a person; however, I needed to write a review. I decided to write something simple: *Jeff stayed with us for two weeks. Nice man.* That's all I could say. I wanted to say that he was high-maintenance, and he should book an apartment or a condo for himself in the future.

In his review of our home, he mentioned the quiet location but that it was only suitable if you didn't plan to cook. I found that amusing since he cooked three meals a day during his stay.

Most experiences will have moments that make you go hmmmm, and you are not going to jive with every guest. Just remember that they are only *temporary* moments in your life.

Recently, I had a gentleman stay with me for a couple of evenings. He appeared to be a great guest, and he communicated well regarding his arrival and stayed quietly to himself. After a recent guest who was extremely challenging, he seemed to be easygoing.

We didn't bump into each other often since we both worked during the day, but on his last morning, we had the chance to visit over tea and coffee. As I walked into the kitchen, I noticed his coffee grounds sitting in the kitchen sink and several empty sugar packets on the beverage platter. It surprised me that he hadn't dumped them in the trash himself.

During our conversation, he reached over and took an overripe banana saying he was going to help himself to one of the bananas since he was hungry.

I said, "Well, it's too bad you won't be here tomorrow. I was going to make banana bread with those bananas."

He didn't even say, "Oops!" He just kept munching away on the banana. Then, instead of throwing away the stringy pieces, he placed them on my ceramic holder where I keep my tea bag. More than slightly irritated now, I picked them up in front of him and threw them out. Then, he proceeded to hand me his banana peel to throw away. He was definitely another case of strange behavior.

It's during these encounters where I rely on everything I've learned about letting it go, being patient, and giving the guest some grace since they are the ones who are traveling. While not every guest is easy, and you will have some difficult ones, it's important to keep things in perspective.

<u>Key Points to Remember</u>

- You'll have easygoing and problematic guests. Having a challenging guest makes you appreciate the easygoing guests all the more. Keep it in perspective that their time with you is limited, and you never have to accept their booking request again.

- Accept and be excited for any learning opportunities that will occur for you or the guest.

Chapter 13

Nurturing and Serving

Of all the lessons I've taken away from this experience of hosting people in my home, the most poignant is that I genuinely enjoy nurturing and serving people. Prior to taking this journey on, I didn't know that about myself, but it's been a real pleasure getting to know people and finding ways to help them during their stay.

Oftentimes, people are looking for something out of the ordinary to do while they are in the area, and it's fun to help them explore the options. The act of doing guests' laundry is nice because it leaves them more time to do what they came to do in the first place. I know when I'm a guest I find that thoughtful, so I continue to work at finding ways to provide more services for guests.

I think one of the reasons I had such a hard time with Nancy the controlling "roommate" is that she wanted to rule the roost even though she was a temporary guest. Serving or nurturing her seemed impossible, and when I would *try*, she was not appreciative of my efforts or didn't acknowledge it, which was discouraging.

I enjoy hosting people who are relocating to the area because they are interested in learning more about the area and are looking for recommendations regarding neighborhoods, schools, restaurants, and the general location. It's nice to be able to share information on my community and how it's changed. Typically, I can provide some good options for where to begin their search.

Recently, I had a young girl from Pakistan stay with me. She was relocating to the area to work and was looking for a place to live. It was her first day at this company, and she was far from home. When she came back that day, I asked her about her first day at work when she returned. We had a great conversation and when she checked out, she mentioned having a friendly face to come home to and ask how her first day went had meant a lot. Those are the moments that make you happy to be a host.

We've also had opportunities to help guests move their belongings into their new home or offered a ride for a guest who needed to get to the immigration office in time for her appointment. Each opportunity provided us a chance to serve and nurture our guests.

There are many ways to serve or nurture people, and it may be as simple as offering a homemade pastry or a bowl of soup. Equipping guests with an umbrella or something to keep them safe or dry helps them feel safe and cared for while they are away from home. It fills me with pleasure and joy to make these small gestures.

I don't share these stories to put a feather in my cap. I share them to offer my advice to other hosts because when I have people stay with me, I always treat people as I would want to be treated if I was traveling. I like to be able to pass on that favor to other guests. Hopefully, they can pass it on to someone else.

Have you considered the human element of the hosting business you are planning to undertake? As you remember your *why* you want to host guests, also consider that you will engage with people from around the world who bring different disciplines, cultures, and manners. How do you feel about serving people and being available for them? Would you find it rewarding or draining? Would you feel more satisfied serving people intimately in your home or in a separate space? These are important questions to ask yourself before you consider this business prospect.

Key Points to Remember
- Think of what will surprise you most about your hosting journey. The time needed to keep the space clean? The friendships? The fulfilling nature of taking care of people?

- Consider if nurturing or serving your guests will bring you joy. Are you the kind of person who enjoys helping people feel comfortable?

Chapter 14

What are you worth?
Know your worth!

Given my business background, I consider my ROI (Return on Investment) before undertaking any endeavors. I looked at hosting in the same light. Time is a precious commodity and how much you invest in your place and what you decide to list it for is an important consideration.

When I help people consider hosting, they ask, "How much should I list my home or room for on the site?"

I encourage people to look at other listings in the area as if they were looking at comparable home properties for sale. What is the room size? What are they offering? Is it a private or shared bath? You want to make sure your listing is a good comparable for the offering and neighborhood.

I frequently get an email from Airbnb that says a number of people have looked at my rooms but booked elsewhere for between five to twenty-five dollars lower. This happens quite a bit, even during the slow season which generally runs January thru May. There are some hosts who will choose to reduce their prices to get a booking and keep their rooms full. I tend to look at the time and effort involved, and what I'm offering, and decide to pass on reducing my rates significantly. What I'm offering is already a good value for the space and location. What if I lower the rate for a guest who takes an hour-long shower? Or they leave the lights on in the kitchen and entry for several days? There is a cost associated with hosting no matter what kind of space you choose to rent. Keep this in mind!

I have a strict cancellation policy. If you cancel up to so many days ahead of the reservation, then you will not be reimbursed. There are rare occasions where I've made an exception and refunded all or part of a guest's money for the stay. However, recently, I had a guest who booked two weeks in two separate months, and she cancelled each stay only a couple days before her arrival.

On the second cancellation, I didn't refund her money. She waited until the last minute to cancel, and I wasn't able to get anyone in for those two weeks, so I missed that income. In my situation, the Airbnb revenue is not my sole income, but for some people it is. Airbnb hosts are not hotels with an endless stream of incoming customers.

The summer interns send inquiries in February and March in regard to renting for the entire summer. They always ask if I offer a reduced rate for a long-term stay. I decline these reduced-rate requests and politely explain that for the space, location, and amenities, they are getting an excellent value. It never hurts them to ask since I'm sure they are considering their budget for the entire summer and some hosts may honor that type of request.

The best advice for valuing your rental space is to determine what your time and place is worth and have clear boundaries as to what you are willing to accept for your rental. Also consider your *why*. If you have that trip around the world planned soon and you are short on your deposit, perhaps you may want to reduce your rate for a couple of months to try to ensure full bookings. That's the beauty of the site. You determine your price and availability.

<u>Key Points to Remember</u>

- Do your homework and search other host listings in the area to determine demand, value, and pricing. Spend more than one night's worth researching other listings like yours and note the similarities and differences so you can identify what to highlight in your profile, or what services you may want to add to be competitive.

- Remember that more people in and out of your place equals more wear and tear. Items will need to be replaced more often so plan those expenses into your price. Your doormat may get replaced a couple times a year, for instance. You will use more water and electricity if you're renting in your own home.

- Your time is valuable. Don't sell yourself short.

Chapter 15

Be Prepared

I've always been proud of the fact that we have an Eagle Scout in our family. Being prepared has been first and foremost in our home. When we travel, we research the area prior to leaving, pre-book tours to see places of interest, and pack over-the-counter items we may need in an emergency in a foreign country.

However, I've been guilty of forgetting some significant item like a toothbrush or travel-sized toothpaste, especially when I carry the luggage on the plane. So, to make things convenient for our guests, they'll find a basket under the bathroom sink of various travel-sized items for those unpredictable moments. Over the years, I've had several people comment how helpful that is for them and how they appreciated the extra touch.

On the topic of being prepared, I had a guest who was allergic to goose down pillows and wanted me to provide an alternative pillow. I only had one extra pillow in the home at the time, so I purchased several pillows the next day for her and any future guests with the same needs.

Another way we help keep guests prepared is with our information binder in each room that includes helpful information if they are not familiar with the area. As a traveler, I've seen variations of this binder, but I find the following information helpful to include:

- my cell phone number, which is also in their reservation confirmation
- current address
- Wi-Fi network and passcode
- nearest grocery store
- nearest convenience store
- nearest hospital
- nearest pharmacy
- nearest bus stop
- website of the local bus line
- local restaurant recommendations for all budgets
- places of interest
- maps of our area: Redmond and Seattle
- brochures and information for local attractions, museums, and parks
- bike and hiking paths in the area
- best menus for take-out recommendations

There are a lot of other items you could include, and I've had people leave travel information behind with the intent for me to include it in the binder, which I often do.

People will travel to your home from all areas of the world—often from different climates. I have people who visit in the summer and feel cold and need additional blankets. Others arrive in winter, and though we have the heat on, they are not acclimated to the colder weather, so we've provided additional blankets and comforters in the rooms. It's good to show them these extra comforts while checking them in and familiarizing them with the property.

If you choose to become an Airbnb host, remember your main concern will be to prepare for the guests' comfort and safety, even beyond what you might think of for yourself. If there is a concern or need, the best thing to do is to respond immediately with a confirmation that you will be acting on it as soon as possible. As long as the guest knows that you are being responsive, they will be satisfied their concern has been heard.

Key Points to Remember

- Have fun and get creative on the details in your information binder. You are the local expert and should recommend some of your favorite local spots. I try to recommend locally owned places to give our guests a more unique opportunity to experience the area.

- You don't need to go overboard with having a lot of extra stuff available for guests to use. Keep it simple and cover the necessities with a few additional comforts. It will be appreciated.

Chapter 16
Expect the Unexpected

On a typical Seattle morning in March—a cloudy Saturday around forty-five degrees—I woke up early to take our dog, Ginger, out for her morning walk, but I did not enjoy my usual early morning Saturday swim at the local gym. Why? Because I was avoiding the gym and crowds. I never missed a swim unless I was sick or out of town, but we were heading into uncharted territory: a global pandemic. Going out on the weekends was now reserved only for grocery shopping to avoid crowds and keep me and my family safe and healthy.

That morning I had said good-bye to our Australian guest who had been staying with us for a month. She was leaving at just the right time as the situation was deteriorating in Seattle. We had talked the night before and wondered what her entry protocol would be in Australia since her country was just starting to see the signs of COVID-19 appear in their communities. That day, I flipped two guest rooms to prepare for our next arrivals. Little did I know that my Australian friend would be our last guest until May 26, 2020.

I never imagined that our lives would be turned upside down and inside out in such a short time and without a definitive end in sight. I guess that's why we remind ourselves to expect the unexpected. How quickly this virus would deeply affect my city— and the entire world—seemed impossible at the time.

Writing this chapter was also unexpected. My book was finished and in the hands of my publisher. Five months into the pandemic, we discussed adding this chapter to benefit future Airbnb hosts who join the adventure after the world settles down. Though other chapters mention unexpected happenings, I never imagined that a chapter on handling global surprises would be included! But we agreed that sharing my experience during this unprecedented time would provide a beneficial perspective on home sharing during this period and for unexpected events in the future.

For the Airbnb platform, guests, and hosts, this global pandemic has rocked everyone's world. And I have to say, it has not been pretty. Since I live in Seattle, we were ground zero at the beginning of the pandemic. Caught totally off guard, we didn't see this coming. Here's how it happened.

January 21: the first COVID-19 case in the United States was confirmed in Washington state.

February 29: Seattle's King County confirmed the first COVID-19 death in Washington, which was also the first known in the United States. This death occurred at Evergreen Health in Kirkland, WA. Later, dozens of patients reported symptoms at the Life Care Center in Kirkland.

March 1: a local postal service employee tested positive for COVID-19. Schools announced closures, and people swarmed the stores to stock up on toilet paper and supplies.

March 2: COVID-19 death count increased to six.

March 3: death toll increased to nine, and Seattle Mayor Jenny Durkan declared a state of emergency.

March 11: The World Health Organization declared the COVID-19 outbreak a pandemic.

March 16: the total number of COVID-19 cases in Washington reached 904 with forty-eight deaths.

March 18: President Trump said the U.S. would close the Canadian border to non-essential traffic.

March 22: President Trump issued a major disaster declaration for Washington state, which released federal assistance.

March 23: Governor Jay Inslee directed Washington residents to stay home by executive order. An official lockdown took place. We watched people get laid off or placed on furlough all over the city.

After I flipped those rooms on March 7th, I watched cancellations roll in on my calendar in a steady stream. The chaos in the Airbnb community erupted. We had no idea how long this would last. Uncertainty overwhelmed us all.

Hosts around the world had both flexible and strict cancellation policies. Airbnb determined that guests should not be obligated to travel and put their health in jeopardy if they could not get a refund. So, to make the situation fair to all guests, Airbnb allowed all guests to receive a full refund if requested during a specific time period. More than one billion dollars of cancellations flooded the website. This decision overrode the hosts' existing cancellation policies, which prompted a backlash from hosts.

In my situation, my guest income pays for children's college expenses, trips, and home improvements. However, many hosts rely solely on their Airbnb income to subsidize or pay their mortgages in expensive areas of the country. Other hosts have ridden the Airbnb wave and acquired multiple properties to run as a home-sharing business. Imagine their struggles! Numerous YouTube videos popped up overnight offering suggestions for how to maneuver through this time and try to get ahead of the curve and understand Airbnb's next move. These videos provided hosts with inside information, encouragement, and a community to lean on for support and advice.

You may be wondering what Patty and Donna did with their properties during this time since their accommodations are different than mine. Patty retired from her job in Seattle in late 2019 and moved into her beautiful cabin in the woods. She is currently living there full time and gets to be a guest every day of the year. At least for now, she plans to live in her cabin and enjoy this chapter of her life and leave the hosting to others.

Donna, like many other hosts, received cancellation requests from early March 2020 through July 2020. She did not receive any compensation from Airbnb for those cancellations. She decided to stop offering their basement for hosting during that same period because so little was known about the contagion and transmission of the virus.

At one point, she did receive a booking inquiry from a lab technician whose day-to-day work was COVID-19 analysis at the University of Washington, but she was not comfortable with that situation and had to decline the reservation request.

By mid-July, Donna and her husband became more comfortable with measures to protect themselves and the guests and updated the listing to focus on guest safety and cleaning procedures. Donna and her husband stopped the Instant Book feature to maintain the ability to pre-screen guests, and they loosened the cancellation policy to the maximum possible extent. They did not opt into Airbnb's Host Cleaning Protocol because it was too restrictive for them in regard to how the hosts should protect themselves, the length of time that the space should be unoccupied after guest checkout and before guest check-in, and the types of cleaners to be used. When they reviewed reservation requests, they informed guests that if they had experienced symptoms of COVID-19 or have been exposed to COVID-19 in the fourteen days before their stay, guests are asked to cancel their reservation and receive a full refund. No guests have cancelled with those restrictions yet.

Since guests started rebooking in early August, Donna has seen approximately 60-70 percent occupancy while maintaining three days without guests in between bookings. Last but not least, they added candy to the types of snacks they provided for guests because these are stressful times!

As I've mentioned, I have a strict cancellation policy. The reason is, I live in the home I share, so my schedule works around guest arrivals, departures, and maintaining accommodations. If they cancel, it not only disrupts my schedule, but it also means I likely won't have a new booking to replace them immediately. Home-sharing platforms don't have people coming in off the street to book a room like a hotel does. But due to the unique circumstances, I actually favored the refunds, though I wish that Airbnb had been able to notify the hosts prior to notifying the guests. Several other hosts felt the same way.

You might wonder how hosts with multiple properties reacted? They went on the offensive and either pulled their properties from the Airbnb site and went to another home-sharing platform, or they built their own home-sharing platform and invited other hosts to join. Others dropped their rates (sometimes up to 50 percent) just to keep their properties full.

None of those options interested me. I felt that my rooms met the value of my location, and it wasn't my sole income. My rooms could sit empty until this chaos worked itself out, and I would be okay.

When cancellations started dinging my phone, a strange relief washed over me. At the beginning stages of this virus, we had little information on how to combat the situation. Staying isolated as much as possible should stop the spread of the virus, so it was logical that not having guests would keep us and our city safer.

I held out hope that my summer interns would still come to stay with us for several months because both rooms had been booked since the fall of 2019. Unfortunately, even Microsoft and Google eventually stated that all summer interns would be working from their homes this summer. There went the last of my summer bookings. I could not control the circumstances, but I could control what we needed to do to stay safe.

Remember the sayings at the beginning of the pandemic? "Let's do our part so we can eliminate the crowding in the hospitals." "Flatten the curve." I was onboard and we were all in. Not to mention toilet paper and cleaning supplies were difficult to purchase, which would mean keeping guest bathrooms clean could be a challenge. Can you imagine not having any toilet paper to offer?

A recent report from an IPX1031 survey[6] stated that hosts lost $4,046 on average in the first several months that COVID-19 began to spread in the U.S. I can tell you that number is extremely conservative. My own number is triple that amount with a single property.

After the worldwide reports of the backlash from Airbnb hosts, you may have heard about the relief fund that was established to help hosts. According to Business Insider,[7] the relief fund was $250 million. Airbnb created incredibly complicated policies on

6   "Survey Reveals How Airbnb Hosts Are Coping During
         Covid-19." IPX1031, May 15, 2020. https://www.ipx1031.com/
         airbnb-covid/.

7   "Airbnb Will Require 24 Hours between Rentals to Limit
         Spread of COVID-19 | Markets Insider." Business Insider.
         Business Insider, April 28, 2020.

what—if anything—would be refunded and how much a host would receive and when the deposit would arrive. Hosts would receive a certain percentage based on cancelled bookings that fell within a certain time frame. Those time frames changed frequently.

It proved difficult to keep up with their changes. I had many other important things to concern myself with at the time and decided to be grateful for whatever came my way. I received a deposit of $800—a far cry from the revenue I actually lost. I decided to move on and not get worked up about it while being grateful for my current situation. Fortunately, I still had my other career, a safe home, and a healthy family.

After we passed through the cancellation whirlwind that ensured that our summer would be wildly different, we decided to embrace the time we had together and what we could accomplish around the house. You would think I'd have had my fill of cleaning, but ironically, I threw myself into doing the deepest of deep cleans. Not a speck didn't get cleaned or thrown out. The weekends cycled like Groundhog Day. Giving the home some TLC became the focus of the next few months. The pandemic was stressful enough to wrap our heads around, so not having guests to manage during this time turned into a blessing.

Eventually, we did get an inquiry from a young man who was going to school in Arizona and had an internship at Amazon for the summer. His internship was based at home, but he wanted to beat the heat of the Arizona summer and visit some friends in Seattle. We talked at length about his level of exposure to the virus, coming up to Seattle, and the new expectations in the home as a result of COVID-19. Given that the guest would be in my shared home, I felt that asking more specific questions about his trip, plans, and potential exposure to the virus were best for all of us. After all, he would be coming in and out of the home, using the kitchen, and sharing a restroom.

He didn't seem to mind and took the questioning

in stride, while being understanding. Perhaps he was relieved that we were taking the situation so seriously. We were all doing the best we could with the information we had at the time. He agreed to the new house rules and booked a stay beginning on May 26.

Prior to his arrival, I set up various cleaning stations to help keep the home safe and clean. In the kitchen, I designed a small poster with a series of cleanliness steps to keep cleaning consistent for everyone.

Wash hands when entering kitchen.
Rinse all dishes and put in the dishwasher.
Use disinfectant wipes to wipe down the kitchen counters.
Wipe down the fridge and microwave handles.
Wipe down the kitchen light switch.
If you touched it, wipe it.

You might think that this is all common sense. Yes, it is. But I can tell you that a majority of people do not do any of these steps when using the kitchen. Though it may seem like overkill, posting some cleaning rules to keep everyone safe during a pandemic couldn't hurt one bit. I also put a sign by the front door to remind guests to wipe the handles and placed some wipes nearby as well.

Currently, I do not require people to wear masks in the house. They are welcome to if they like, but I don't want to create an uncomfortable or unfriendly environment by mandating it. We are still learning more about the virus, so beyond the printing of this chapter who knows what will become common after this.

Some friends thought I was crazy to let someone in my home during this pandemic. But at the end of May, we were months into this unique situation and were far more informed, so it seemed like the right time to cautiously move forward. We could not live in what I call the "COVID cocoon" forever. At some point, we had to accept our circumstances and learn how to pivot and adapt. Booking this first guest did just that. We moved in faith that things would be okay.

Airbnb established a new cleaning policy for hosts, and they had a small online training course with a quiz at the end. One suggestion was to wait a minimum of twenty-four hours in between bookings to limit possible COVID-19 transmissions.[8] Many of us hosts are continuing to adhere to that. The new cleaning protocol is lengthy, but it's nearly identical to my existing checklist that I've always used for each room flip. I still offer the same level of detailed cleaning now as I was prior to the pandemic. One easy change is that I now use gloves when I strip the bedding, towels, and clean the room. Those nitrile gloves are my new best friend.

When my guest checks in, they'll find hand sanitizer in the room and disinfectant wipes. Whatever they may need to feel more comfortable, we are willing to provide—including extra toilet paper since it's fully restocked again! People have different levels of comfort, and it's easy to accommodate if you have a great customer service attitude.

Our guest from Arizona did arrive on May 26, and he was a delight to host. He participated in our daily cleaning protocol, which included wiping down surfaces in the kitchen with disinfectant wipes. He seemed empathetic to our situation as hosts during a pandemic. His easy-going nature was really helpful and pleasant for our first pandemic guest. He asked if he could have his friends over to our home during our initial discussions, and I told him that we would not be able to accommodate since we wanted to minimize our exposure by avoiding having groups of people in the home.

---

8   https://markets.businessinsider.com/news/stocks/airbnb-24-hours-between-rentals-limit-covid-spread-2020-4-1029139570.

Since we started hosting, that eleven-week stretch was the longest period that we did not have a guest in our home. After our Arizona guest, our rooms started booking with more frequency again, though often at short notice.

Moving forward with Airbnb, we hosts are learning as we go. At the start of the pandemic, I joined an online group where we could share and seek advice from each other since each day changed with the pandemic and Airbnb directives. Sometimes this group provided the best information we needed as some members were insiders to Airbnb. We are still sharing tips as we move forward, but now we discuss how the guests and their expectations have changed and how best to adapt.

In resort communities, the hosts are booking people who would normally stay at a resort but prefer to stay in a home or condo because there is less exposure to crowds. These guests have a different level of expectations, which has offered new challenges for hosts. The guests typically feel more entitled and have different expectations that would normally be filled with positions such as bell hops, concierges, and room service. Both sides have felt frustration with the new situations. Airbnb accommodations are not resorts with twenty-four-hour amenities.

Just as hosts are having to adapt, new Airbnb guests will also need to adapt. One suggestion has been to clearly clarify on your booking page that some of these commonly expected resort amenities are not included in your home. Ensuring that all parties understand the expectations up front can really make a difference for guests to be happy.

For the host who has multiple listings, it's been especially difficult. Some of them have switched from short-term monthly rentals to long-term yearly rentals, but it's been incredibly hard for them to make it work. With properties sitting empty, cash flow running dry, and people not traveling, maintaining multiple properties has made it impossible to meet their financial commitments. The first step for some hosts was to reduce nightly rates to attract visitors. Ultimately, some have had to lay off staff and lose their offices. One host used to be a real estate broker, and he has returned to that career to make ends meet.

I know that many hosts pulled their homes off the platform or went dormant. As a traveler myself, I looked for a short weekend getaway, craving a change of scenery. We reached out to several hosts. Their homes were available on the site, but they declined our request by stating that they will not be hosting for the remainder of the year. Searching for the right place only to be told it never planned to be available felt so frustrating. Everyone is working through this the best they can and dealing with different sets of circumstances. Fortunately, I don't have a family member with a compromised immune system or my story would be different.

Airbnb will find their way back to being as strong and as innovative as ever. In March of 2020, this company, which was poised to go public, faced a multitude of cancellations and their revenue dissolved overnight. It came as no surprise when they announced in May that the company would be laying off 25 percent of their workforce.

The layoffs have created longer wait times on the telephone help line. I had a situation in early July that needed immediate attention regarding a current guest booking, and I waited on the phone for forty-five minutes before someone picked up my call. Perhaps there is a silver lining for Airbnb in that this will make Airbnb go back to its roots: attracting travelers who are looking for a more hospitality-based approach where the emphasis is on community, relationships, and experiences during their stay. The world of travel may change, but people still want to feel that connection when they travel. I suspect with the appropriate leadership, Airbnb can take a great concept with a solid foundation and make it work again.

Airbnb's Go Near campaign has had a positive impact for people like me who are looking to get out of the house for a weekend but not venture too far. Many remote properties outside of town like the beach, the mountains, and lakeside getaways have become attractive for local travelers. Overall, Airbnb has a better chance of being able to adapt what's happening to the needs of the consumer, compared to an overcrowded hotel chain which could be slower to react and employ new strategies globally.

It's unknown as to what will happen with the virus and our global economy. As some of the cash-strapped hosts with multiple properties leave the site, we could see more people like myself renting individual rooms for extra cash on the side. That's just sheer speculation as things can always change, and I've learned to expect the unexpected!

People are still looking for a personal and unique experience when traveling, and I have already seen that there will be a continued desire to book Airbnb listings. Airbnb and their hosts have learned a lot during this period. I'm continuing to put my trust in the organization and the platform.

If someone were to come to me today and ask if hosting is still a good idea, I'd ask them those same questions we discussed at the beginning of the book, primarily, what is your *why*? Your *why* is going to get you through any pandemic, rough patch with a guest, or changes coming from Airbnb. Our ability to be able to host people in our home has afforded additional financial security and the irreplaceable opportunity to meet a lot of wonderful people from all over the world. For that, I am eternally grateful.

<u>Key Points to Remember</u>

- Always know that your situation hosting can change at any time. Relying solely on Airbnb for your sole source of income is risky, just as any business can be. Be diverse and have multiple streams of income.

- You call the shots for your home's availability. The beauty of the Airbnb platform is that you can pull yourself off completely or make your room/home available at any time. This pandemic is proof that you can still be a part of the community, and the availability of your place matches your comfort and availability.

- Sharing in the Airbnb community is key between hosts. We learned so much from each other during the pandemic. Openly sharing why, how, and what we were doing became critical for feeling safe, being heard, and finding solutions. Email, Facebook, and YouTube were great ways for us to stay connected and in front of what was happening globally and in our community.

- Never run out of toilet paper and cleaning supplies! Always stay stocked up. You never know when an emergency will wipe out the stores.

- Buckle your seatbelt and hang on for the ride. We felt like we were on a roller coaster. It's been one wild ride. Be flexible, understanding, and aware.

Chapter 17

Getting Started Checklist for Home Sharing

Since I'm often asked how to get started as an Airbnb host, I thought it would be helpful to provide a checklist. These bullet points could easily make their own chapter, but I'll keep it simple here. These tips will help you be successful from the start, and you can implement any that feel comfortable for you.

- **Be honest about your listing.** When describing your property online, paint a realistic picture of your space for guests with varying needs who will arrive at different hours of the day. If there are three flights of stairs to climb to get to the front door, add that information. You don't want people to be surprised, especially a person with a disability. If you have a dog, make sure to share that information clearly to help people with severe allergies know to look for another property.
- **Take good pictures.** Enlist the help of a photographer to take pictures of your home so they can utilize their skills to ensure proper lighting and staging to make your home look spectacular. Be sure you capture the room amenities like desks and chairs in

each room. It's fun to photograph the bundle of lavender and soaps in the bathroom, but the guest is more interested about having the necessary items they will need to have a comfortable stay. I've learned people will base their decision to stay at a certain Airbnb by only looking at the pictures in a listing. I've done it myself, too. If the place looks run down or dirty, then I'm quick to move on. Have a critical eye as you decide which photographs to use in your profile.

- **Do more than you promise in the listing.** Remember that element of surprise? Have a unique welcome routine or provide a small gift or item for your guest upon arrival or departure that they will least expect.
- **Send your guests a pre-arrival email one week prior to their arrival**. Don't make them reach out to you. Provide as much detail as needed to your guest concerning how to find the home or how to check in after hours. If they take public transportation, provide them the link for the best way to get to your property. Anticipate their needs. Airbnb is testing a feature to allow hosts to create and manage scheduled messages that is expected sometime in 2021.
- **Information binder.** Put together a manual for the house that includes house rules, pertinent info, and local attractions. If there are appliances that are tricky to operate, then create some laminated instructions to place by the item.
- **Personally greet your guests**. This is the ideal situation but may not happen every time. If you can't be there to greet them, reach out the next day and ask if there is anything they need to make their stay more comfortable. This lets them know that you are available and attentive to their needs.

- **Offer a special gift in the room at check-in.** Provide some chocolates, water or small gift basket. Remember, they've been traveling and may appreciate some bottled water or a granola bar without having to ask or be worried that they didn't have time to stop at a store.
- **Have a self-check-in process.** Make sure you communicate the process clearly and that it's easy to follow. The fewer steps the better.
- **Update your space.** If your furniture is worn out, take time to replace it. Make sure that the guest living space is clean and tidy, and the drawers and closets are empty. Nothing makes a guest more uncomfortable than when they must hang up their clothes next to your items.
- **Provide access to charging outlets.** Provide plenty of outlets for computers and electronics. Most people travel with several devices. If your room has a limited number of outlets, increase them by purchasing adapters or power strip cords that offer three or six outlets in one.
- **Desk and chair.** Make sure you have a good desk and chair in the guest's room with good lighting. This is helpful for any traveler.
- **Toiletries.** Make sure the extra toiletries, hair dryer, and ironing board are easy to find. Their location should also be mentioned in the information binder.
- **Extra blankets and pillows.** Have plenty of these available in an obvious place. Provide a couple of different kinds to accommodate people with various allergies and comfort needs.

- **Coffee and tea.** Make sure the beverage service is set out and convenient to use. I put mine on a tray so that all of the choices are together. If we don't have guests, it can easily be removed from our kitchen counter and put away.
- **Wi-Fi code.** Leave this information in an obvious place. It can be in your binder or printed and put in a frame on the guest's desk. This is one of the first questions I get when people check in. They must be able to be connected to their devices!
- **Smoke detector, carbon monoxide detector, and fire extinguisher**. Make sure you have each of these devices in the home, and they operate correctly. Check batteries on a regular basis. Write the location of the fire extinguisher in the binder or make a simple map to show them. Keep baking soda in an obvious place near the stovetop to help put out any grease fires.
- **Lock up your valuables**. Have a system for locking items and make sure it's a consistent practice. If in doubt about whether or not you value something enough to lock it away, consider how you'd feel if it was taken. When in doubt, lock it away.
- **Toilet plunger.** I've said it before and I'll say it again. Have a plunger by every toilet. You don't need to be awakened after midnight for something they could have done themselves. It also saves the guest the embarrassment.
- **Have fun**. Enjoy your guests and make new friends!

<u>Key Points to Remember</u>

- This is your unique space. Customize and make it available to your guests however you see fit.

- Enjoy the journey!

Chapter 18

Oh, the Places We've Stayed

My family and I have had fun experiencing other Airbnb listings, and ultimately, it's helped me become a better host by seeing different places and how each host made their place a unique experience. You can incorporate some of these ideas as they suit you and your property.

Earlier I mentioned the tiny house listing where we had a memorable experience of taking a short ferry to Guemes Island for a weekend stay. We had been curious about tiny house living, so we thought this would be a fun opportunity to give it a try. This artist couple built their own tiny house and put it on the lower lot of their property. Everything was first class in the home.

Guemes is a tiny island and there are not a lot of extra amenities, so we brought all of our food. It felt like a luxury camping trip! They offered the use of their beautiful deck on the main house and a fire pit that we enjoyed as well. Our first attempt at tiny house living was a success, and we loved it.

Another memorable listing was the replica wildfire lookout tower in Tiller, Oregon. This tower is so popular now that it's almost impossible to get a reservation at this prized spot. The two hosts offered a slice of heaven in a remote area of southern Oregon. Again, we brought our own food, but we enjoyed a beautiful four days exploring the area, seeing

Crater Lake, and rafting the Rogue River. We shared many host stories, and my son made a drone video for them to use as they liked. We really enjoyed the space and the chance to get to know the hosts. I know for certain that they love hosting people from anywhere in the world.

My friend and I had the pleasure of visiting Salt Spring Island in British Columbia this past summer, and we stayed in a cottage that one could only dream of owning. This lovely place high in the mountains overlooked the Canadian Gulf Islands, high enough that we felt removed from the hustle and bustle of life. The vista of the British Columbia ferries coming and going during sunrise and sunset made for unforgettable memories. We were so fortunate to stay at such a beautiful location.

Recently, we chose to be brave and stayed overnight in a sailboat in La Conner, Washington. The unique, rustic sailboat made us grateful we had only booked it for one evening. It was one of those listings that had not been kept up, and the host wasn't in the business of making you feel comfortable. However, it was an experience, and that's what we were looking for that weekend.

My daughter and I had some great experiences traveling overseas to London and Paris. In England, we rented a flat in a quaint village close to Nottingham—an area we might not have explored had it not been for this cozy flat. The neighborhood grocery and restaurants charmed us immensely, and by the end of the trip, we had favorite places to shop and eat. In Paris, we rented a room in a gentleman's home for a couple of evenings. He was quite charming and helped us with our plans. We had arrived by train from London and were running late for a private food tour with my favorite food blogger. Our host took the time and walked us to the Métro, helped us buy our tickets, and made sure we got on the right train so we would make the tour on time. Had he not helped us, I know we would have been late and kept our guide waiting. Our host also provided a beautiful breakfast every morning for us to enjoy—an unexpected surprise.

While taking my daughter on a road trip to graduate school at Oklahoma State, we used Airbnb for several stops along the way. We stayed in Boise, Idaho and Salt Lake City, Utah, and both listings were comfortable, quiet, and offered air conditioning.

We drove beyond our planned stop in Denver and decided to use some credit card points at a national hotel chain. The experience wasn't nearly as nice or comfortable as it had been in the other two locations. The hotel lacked that personal touch and comfort that you feel when you are staying in a place where the host has spent a lot of time and pride to get ready for your arrival.

We also stayed in a charming home in San Francisco and had the opportunity to chat with the host. She offered a comfortable space for three people and an outdoor patio to sit at in the morning. For a Seattle person, this was a luxury given the time of year. The kitchen was well equipped, and she offered a lot of breakfast and snack items that were truly over the top and unexpected.

We look forward to more adventures with fun hosts in picturesque places. Are you inspired to become a host yet?

Key Points to Remember

- Learn from other hosts. Get out there and stay in some listings in your area or abroad. There's no better way to learn how to improve your own space than by seeing other places and talking with other hosts.

- Look for small details at each place you stay, even when you're visiting a friend. Perhaps there's a detail or an item like a fire pit that you'd like to incorporate into your own rental.

Chapter 19

What's Next on the Horizon?

During the process of writing this book it's been fun to reflect on my progression during this home-sharing journey. I remember how nerve-racking the anticipation of that first guest was and how I wanted to make sure things went just perfectly. Overall, I've found people are pretty forgiving if they see you are genuine in your intent to host well and can feel the warmth of your hospitality.

I often wonder what's next for our family and how much longer we'll be offering our home to weary travelers. It's been a rewarding experience, but at the same time, I can see it taking a toll on our home and our family. It's important to schedule those breaks to allow some privacy and a chance to recharge as a normal family.

I once had a delightful guest who wanted to come back to Redmond to visit her son over the holidays and asked to stay with us. As much as I wanted to welcome her to our home, I needed to have that family time during the holidays.

Overall, we don't conduct ourselves any differently when we have guests, but my son said something the other day that struck a chord. He said, "Mom, it's been nice not having any guests this week. I can yell for you when I need you and not have to worry if I'm bothering anyone." Someday my kids will be out of the house and on their own, and I'll miss hearing them holler "Mom" to get my attention.

When I'm cleaning between guests, I look at the rooms that once were my rooms, but they don't feel like my rooms anymore. Even though I love my home and take pride in maintaining it, I'm beginning to detach myself from it. Maybe this was the plan for me to eventually be able to sell my home once my kids had moved on so I can create my own new adventures. Or perhaps, I'll keep it and rent the entire space on Airbnb.

I know that hosting people is not completely out of my future. During the 70s, I often stayed at bed-and-breakfasts while traveling. I read numerous books on the business and thought one day, that would be fun to do. Who would have guessed that I'd be doing a version of it now? I have toyed with the idea of having my own bed-and-breakfast and looked at several options, but have determined that it's not my time yet. I have a lot more places to go and things to experience before I go down that path.

Ultimately, what I have learned is that I do enjoy meeting people and making sure they are happy, comfortable, and nurtured. I love to surprise them in the morning with something completely unexpected like homemade scones. To see people appreciate how much you've put into your place to make them comfortable is rewarding. I hope you'll join me in this amazing venture of hosting other travelers!

Our Favorite Banana Bread Recipe

Since I referenced my banana bread a couple of times in my book, I had to share it with you. Hope you enjoy!

Sour Cream Banana Bread

Ingredients:
1 stick or ½ cup of butter
1 cup sugar
2 eggs, beaten
1½ cup flour
1 tsp baking soda
½ tsp salt
1 cup mashed bananas (approx. 3)
½ cup sour cream
1 tsp vanilla
1 cup walnuts, chopped

Directions:
Preheat oven to 350 degrees. Grease and flour one 9-inch loaf pan. In a large bowl, cream the butter and sugar until light and fluffy. Add the eggs and combine. Whisk together the flour, baking soda, and salt. Combine with the butter mixture. Add the sour cream, bananas, vanilla, and walnuts and stir well. Pour into the prepared pan and bake for 50 minutes. Cool for 10 minutes, then remove the loaf and place it on a wire rack to continue cooling.

Acknowledgements

I would like to thank Nancy Burkhalter, who was my writing coach in the beginning. She encouraged me to just keep writing! Also, Brie Greenhalgh for helping me with the editing of the book so it was ready to promote! To my friends and family who have listened to my stories over the years, thank you! Through many walks and talks, you've heard these stories before they were printed. I'm thankful to have such an amazing group of friends and a family that's always believed in me and supported my journey.

My sincere thanks to Brittiany Koren of Written Dreams Publishing for helping me to launch this book, and to the designers, Ed Vincent, Katy Brunette, and Maria Connor for the extra work you put in on *The Tell-All Guide to Airbnb Hosting* to make it perfect. Thank you to A.L. Mundt for her excellent copy-editing, and a special thank you to Craig Larsen for taking photos to include on the cover.

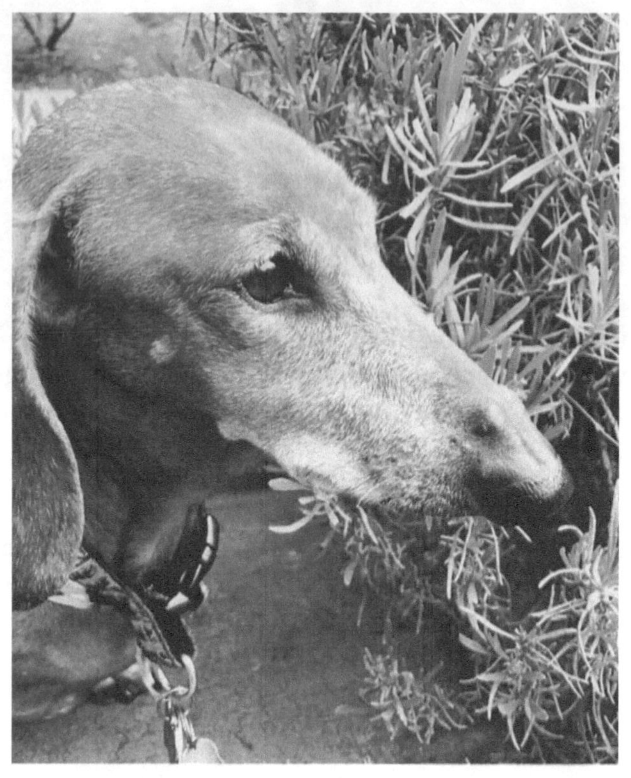

The most important host in our home, Ginger, went over the rainbow bridge on April 30, 2021, and unfortunately, did not see the printing of this book. Ginger was a loved member of our family, and our guests thoroughly enjoyed giving her affection and "treats."

About the Author

Along-time resident of Redmond, Washington, Deborah Voll is the mother of two independent adult children and one senior dachshund. Opening her own home to home-sharing guests has changed her life for the better as she has befriended guests from around the world and grown through the many adventures that arise. Her vast experiences with guests of all kinds during her many years as an Airbnb Superhost offer readers a wealth of knowledge about hosting on the Airbnb platform and successfully launching their own hosting business. *The Tell-All Guide to Airbnb Hosting* is her first nonfiction book.

Deborah's primary day job navigates the world of manufacturing as she provides products and services to other manufacturing companies. These skills have helped her focus on guest satisfaction and the profitability of her venture with Airbnb. In 2019, Deborah launched her life coaching business along with a weekly podcast called Calm the Chaos. Her coaching business fulfills her passion of caring for others as she helps empower women in midlife to find their own passion and purpose.

When Deborah is not flipping rooms for guests or improving the lives of her coaching clients, you can find her updating her garden, staying active with friends, baking delicious treats for family and friends, or exploring a new city as an Airbnb guest herself. Find her on Instagram @deborahvoll.lifecoach, Facebook, or on her websites: deborahvoll.com and author.deborahvoll.com.

www.ingramcontent.com/pod-product-compliance
Lightning Source LLC
Chambersburg PA
CBHW022109050726
47591CB00002B/739